HOW TO DRAW CATS AND KITTENS

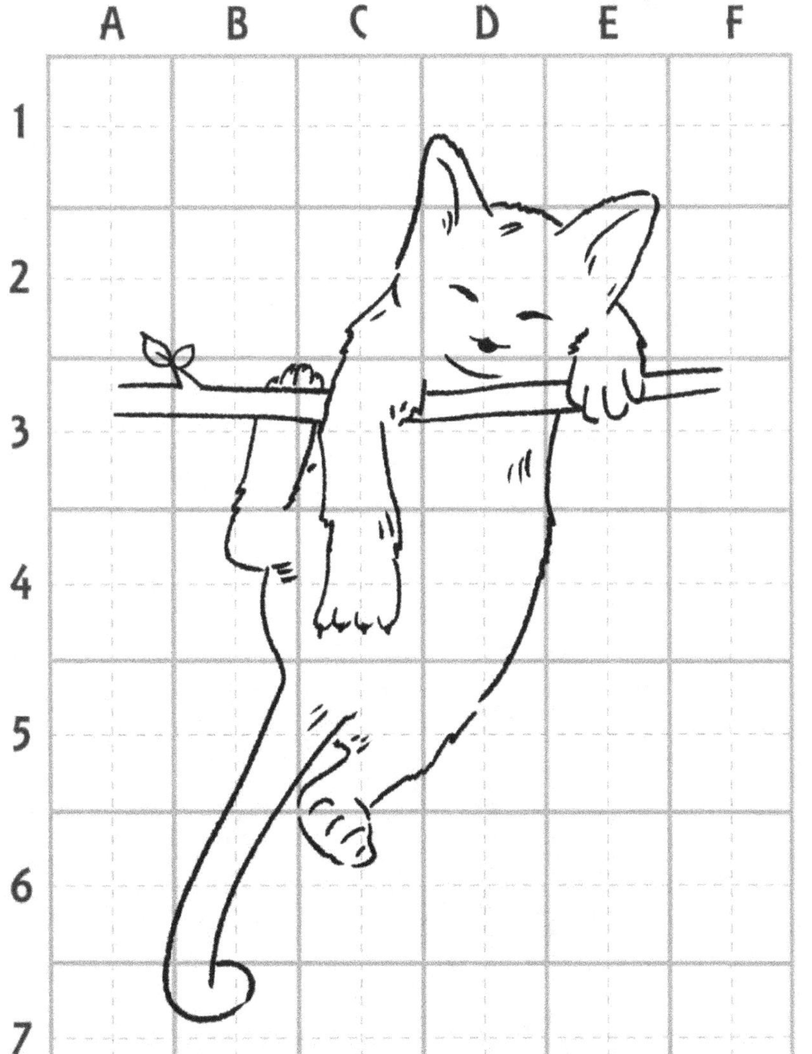

FOR KIDS

Learn To Draw

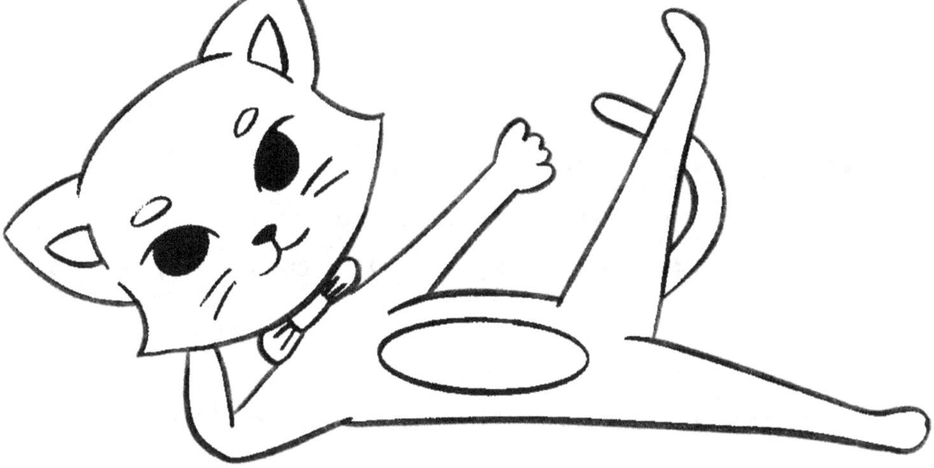

Tips For Drawing:

1. Always use a Pencil. You can always go back and erase or darken your strokes.
2. Focus on what you are doing. Take it easy, slow down and take your time.
3. Draw an outline first, then later you can add details and color too.
4. The most important tip that you have to keep in mind is that *Drawing Takes Time* because it's a skill and it needs Practice!

You Are an Artist

Learn To Draw

Learning to draw is easy with the Grid Method. It has been used for years! It's a great way to work on your drawing skills.

Drawing becomes easier with the grid method since it breaks down the entire image into smaller boxes so that you can focus only on one part or box of the image.

Focus on one box at a time

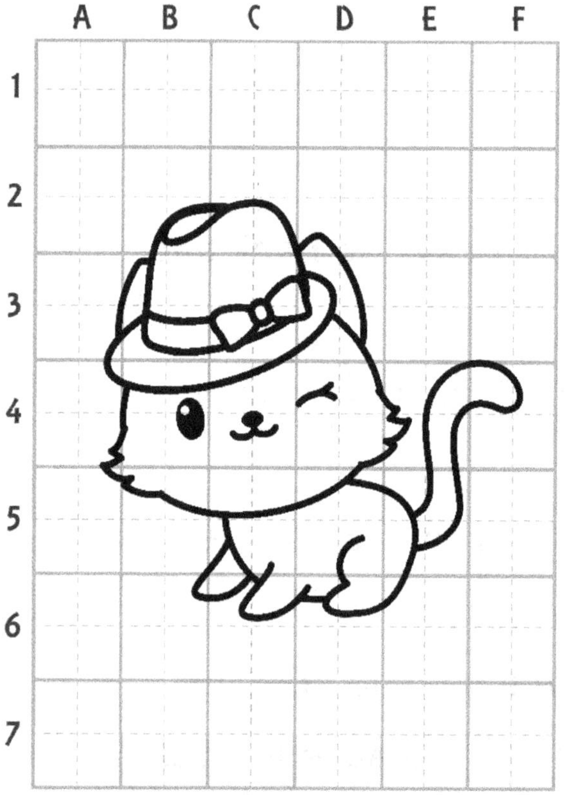

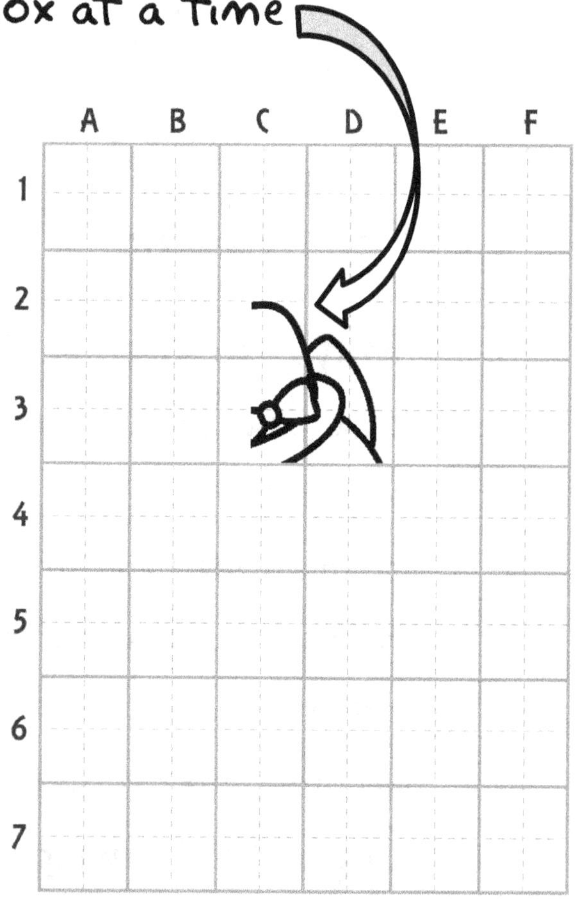

Draw and Color

You Are an Artist

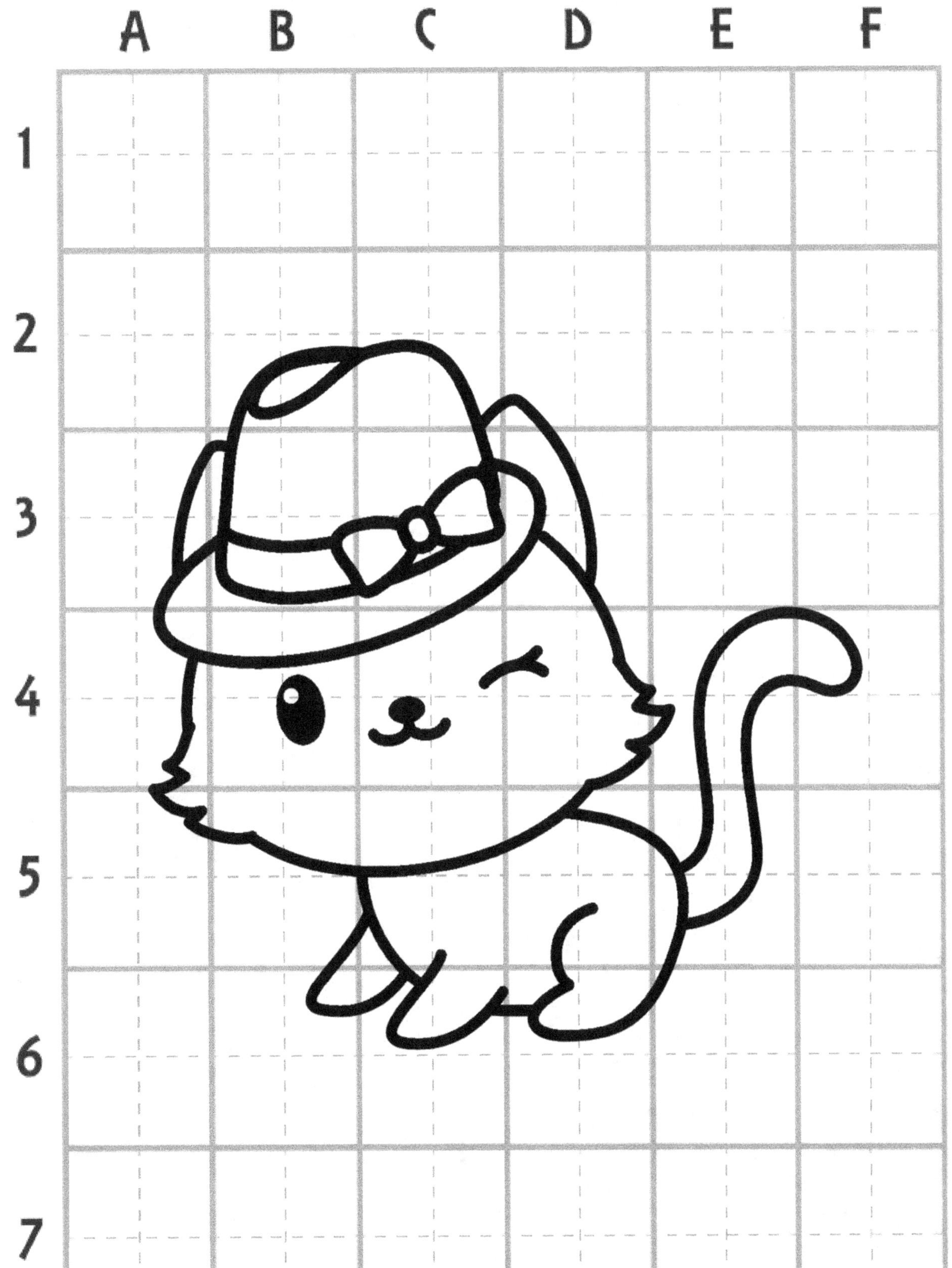
A
B
C
D
E
F
1
2
3
4
5
6
7

Your Turn!

	A	B	C	D	E	F
1						
2						
3						
4						
5						
6						
7						

Practice Makes Perfect!

Draw & Color

Practice Makes Perfect!

Draw & Color

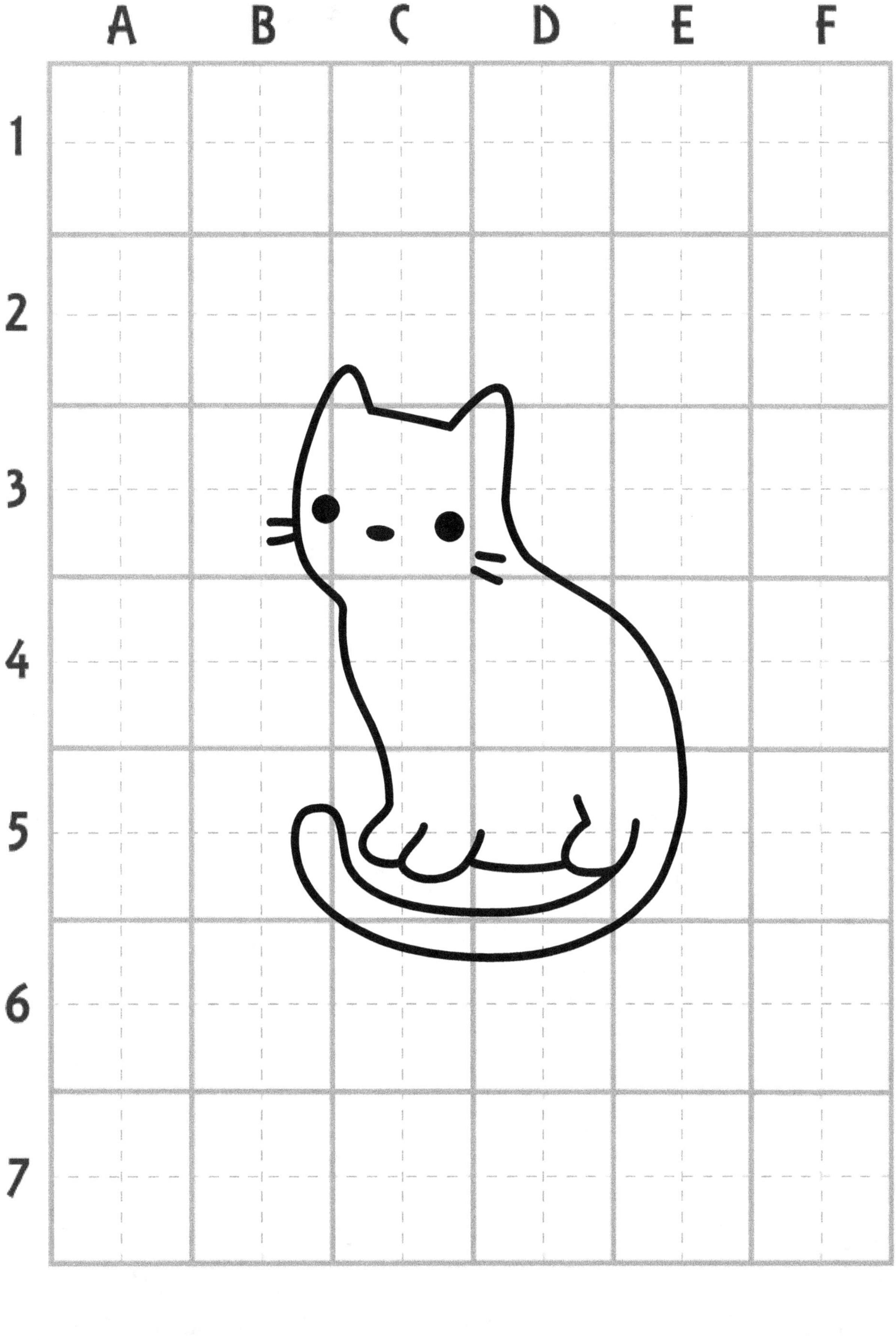
A
B
C
D
E
F
1
2
3
4
5
6
7

Your Turn!

	A	B	C	D	E	F
1						
2						
3						
4						
5						
6						
7						

Practice Makes Perfect!

Draw & Color

Practice Makes Perfect!

Draw & Color

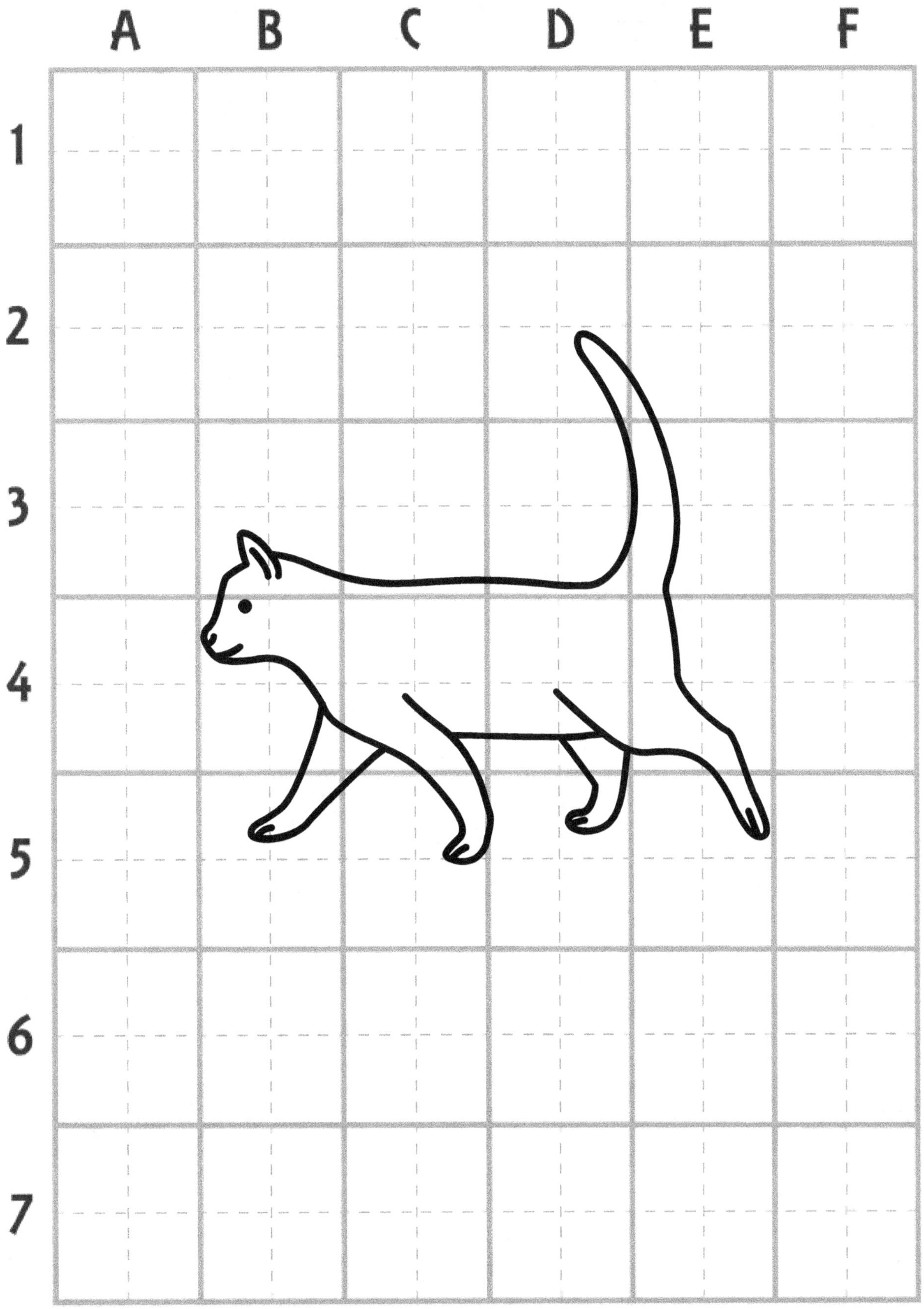
A B C D E F
1 2 3 4 5 6 7

Your Turn!

	A	B	C	D	E	F
1						
2						
3						
4						
5						
6						
7						

Practice Makes Perfect!

Draw & Color

Practice Makes Perfect!

Draw & Color

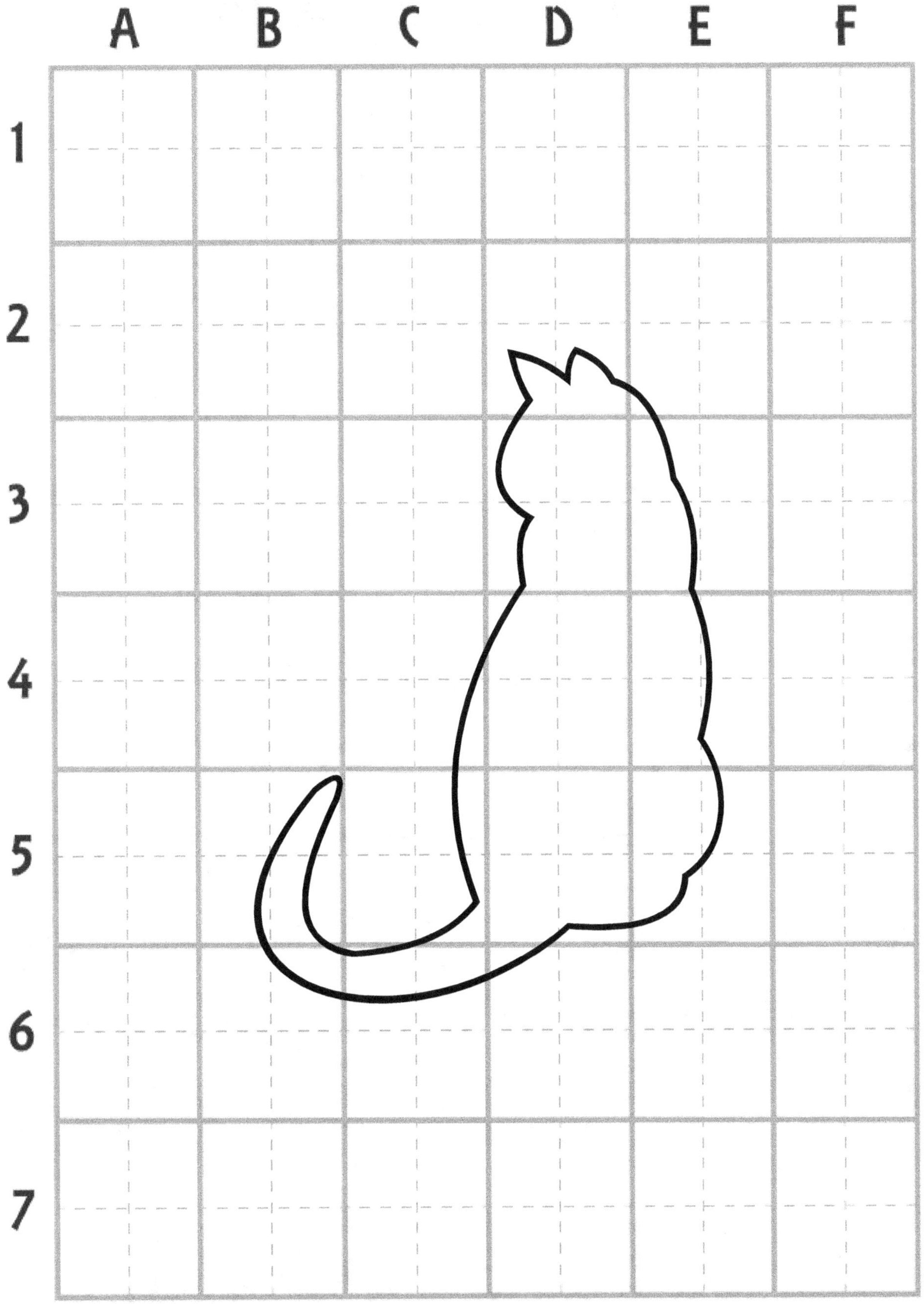
A
B
C
D
E
F
1
2
3
4
5
6
7

Your Turn!

	A	B	C	D	E	F
1						
2						
3						
4						
5						
6						
7						

Practice Makes Perfect!

Draw & Color

Practice Makes Perfect!

Draw & Color

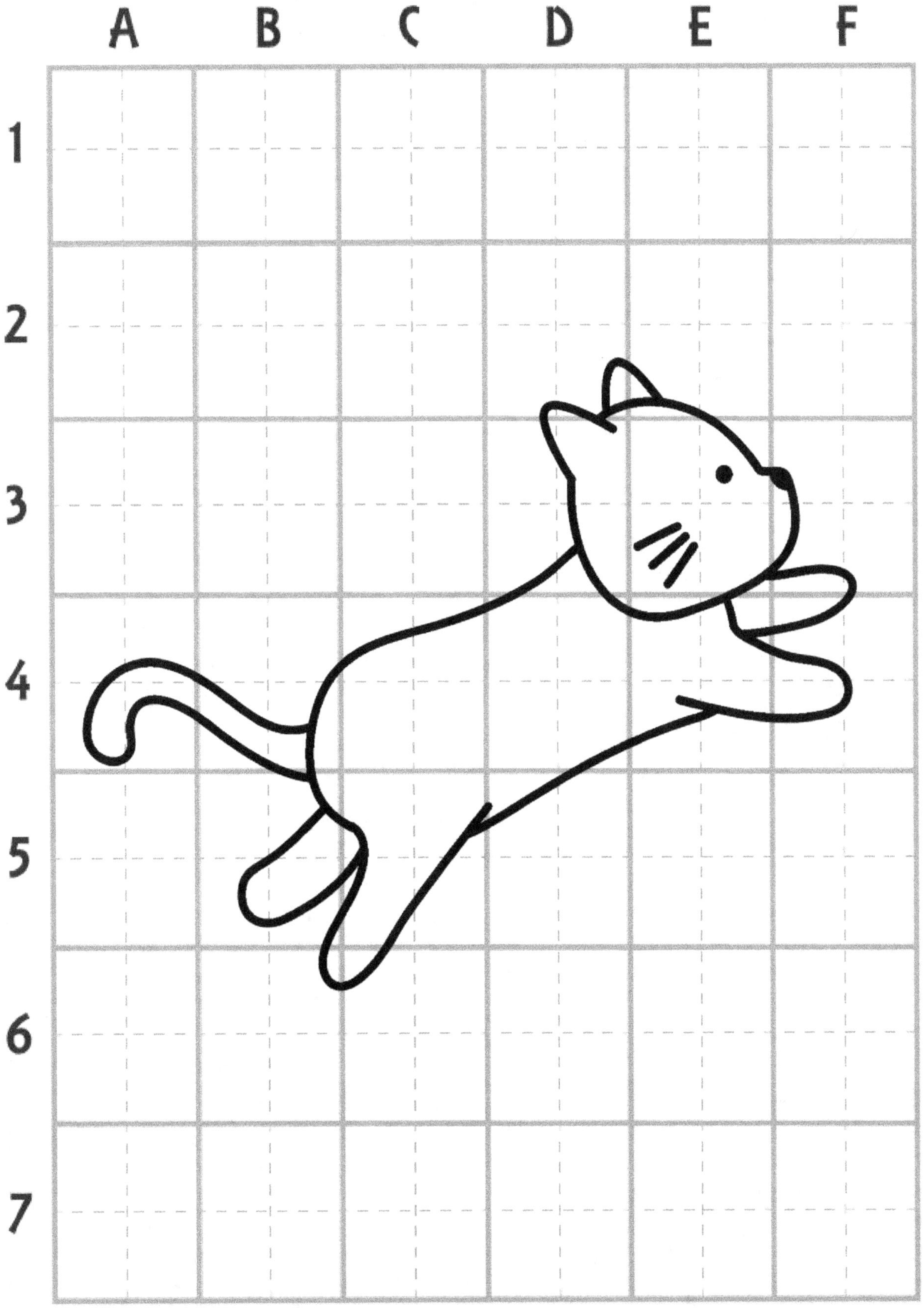
A
B
C
D
E
F
1
2
3
4
5
6
7

Your Turn!

	A	B	C	D	E	F
1						
2						
3						
4						
5						
6						
7						

Practice Makes Perfect!

Draw & Color

Practice Makes Perfect!

Draw & Color

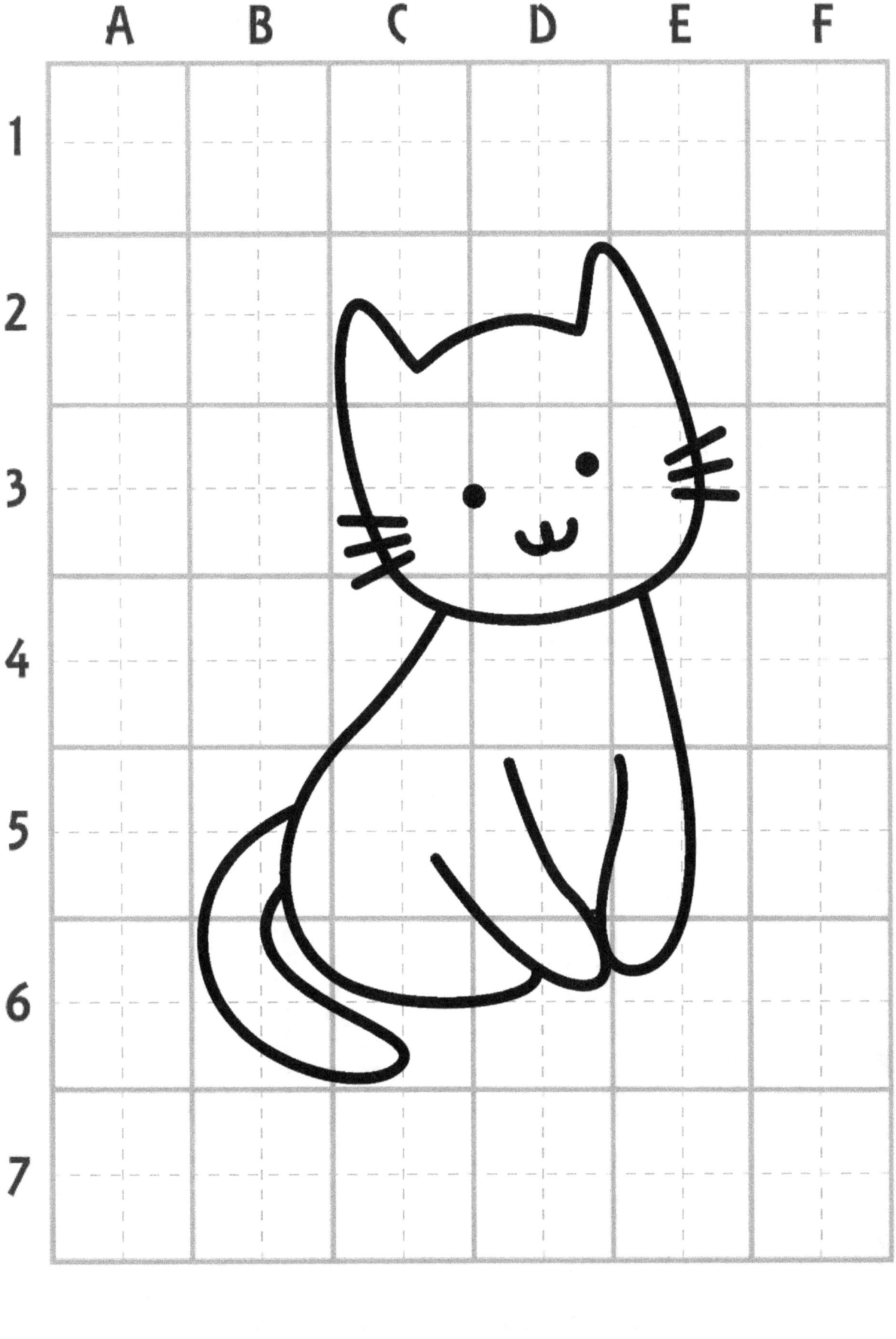
A B C D E F
1 2 3 4 5 6 7

Your Turn!

	A	B	C	D	E	F
1						
2						
3						
4						
5						
6						
7						

Practice Makes Perfect!

Draw & Color

Practice Makes Perfect!

Draw & Color

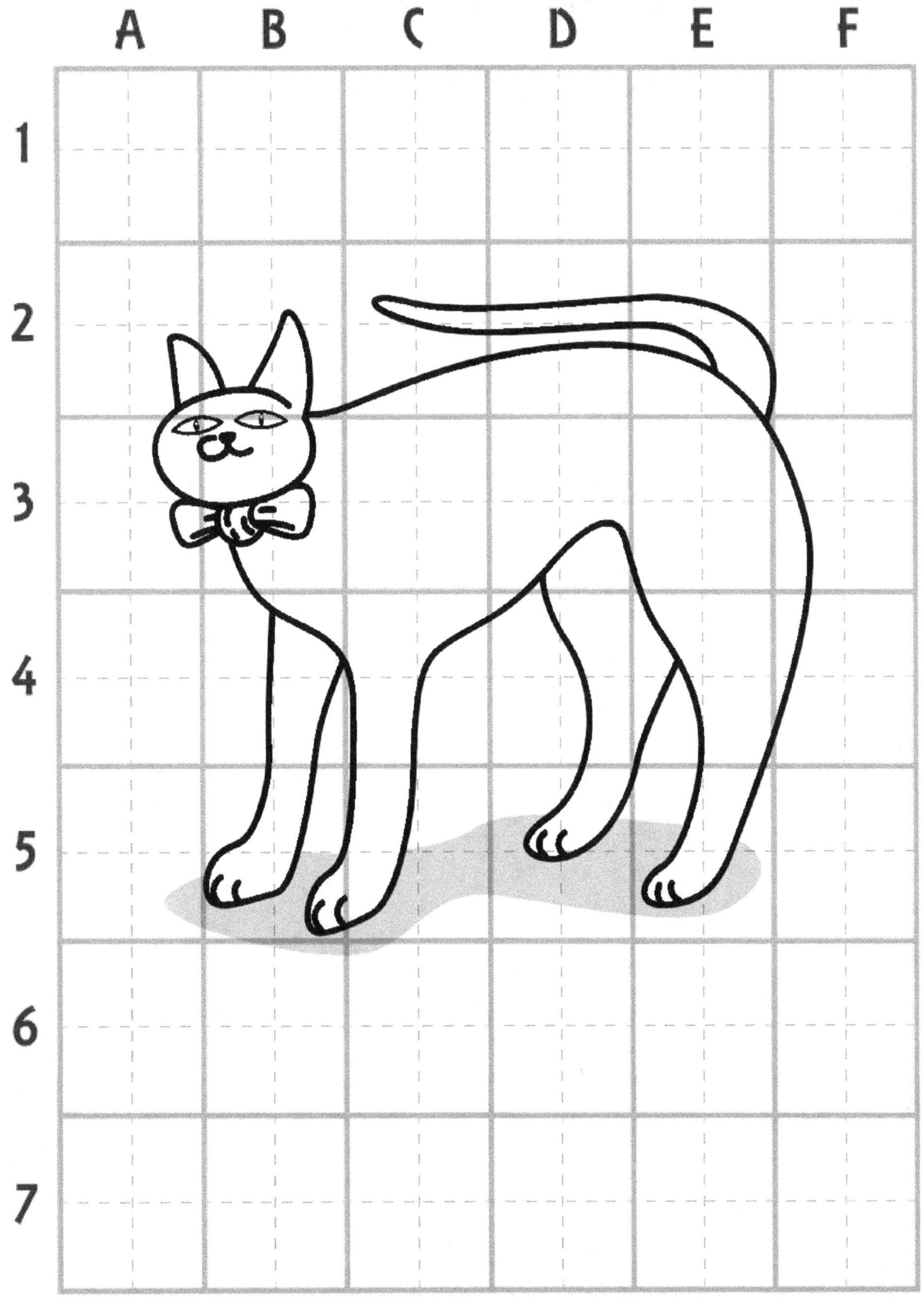
A B C D E F
1
2
3
4
5
6
7

Your Turn!

	A	B	C	D	E	F
1						
2						
3						
4						
5						
6						
7						

Practice Makes Perfect!

Draw & Color

Practice Makes Perfect!

Draw & Color

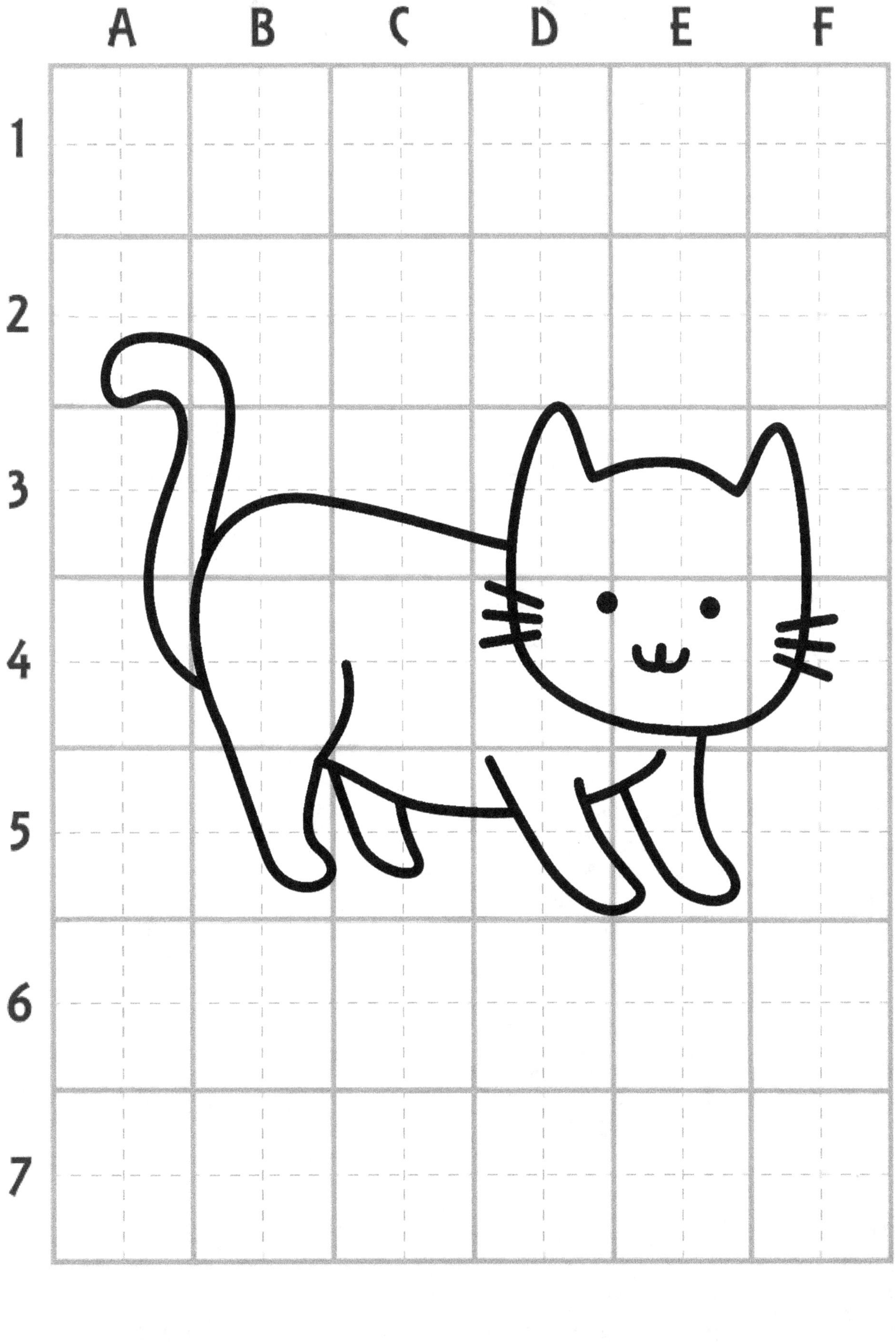
A B C D E F
1
2
3
4
5
6
7

Your Turn!

	A	B	C	D	E	F
1						
2						
3						
4						
5						
6						
7						

Practice Makes Perfect!

Draw & Color

Practice Makes Perfect!

Draw & Color

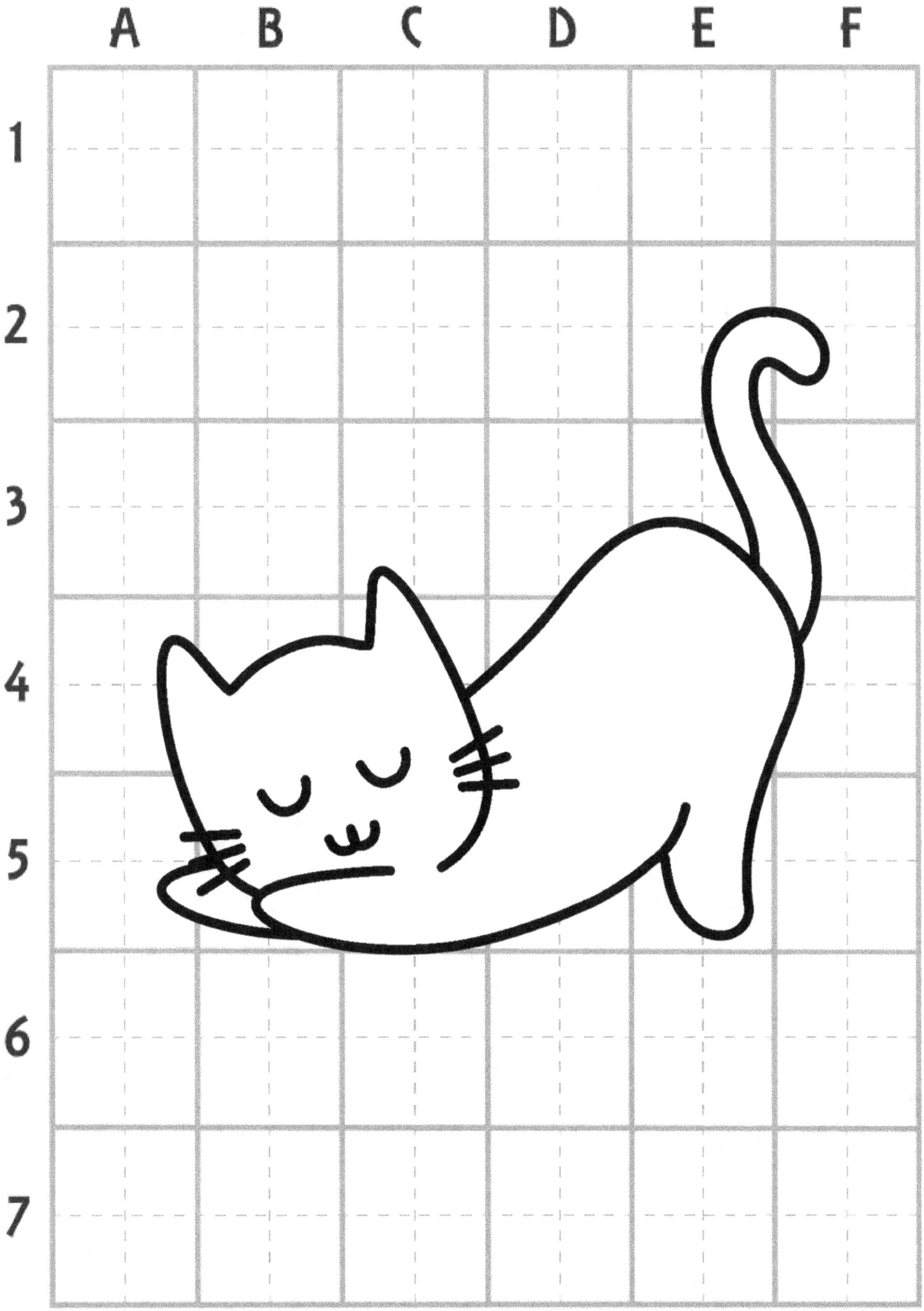
A
B
C
D
E
F
1
2
3
4
5
6
7

Your Turn!

	A	B	C	D	E	F
1						
2						
3						
4						
5						
6						
7						

Practice Makes Perfect!

Draw & Color

Practice Makes Perfect!

Draw & Color

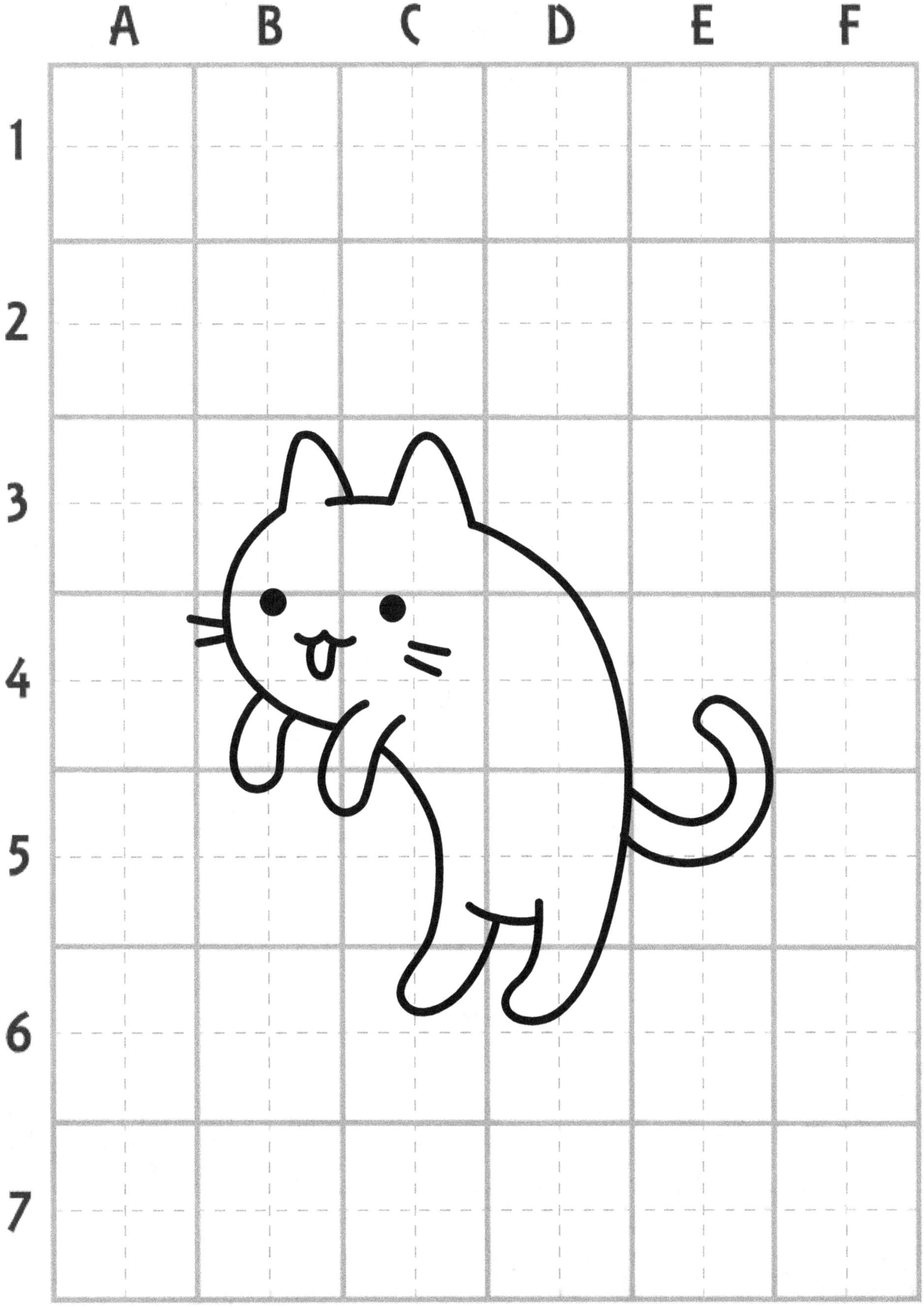
A
B
C
D
E
F
1
2
3
4
5
6
7

Your Turn!

	A	B	C	D	E	F
1						
2						
3						
4						
5						
6						
7						

Practice Makes Perfect!

Draw & Color

Practice Makes Perfect!

Draw & Color

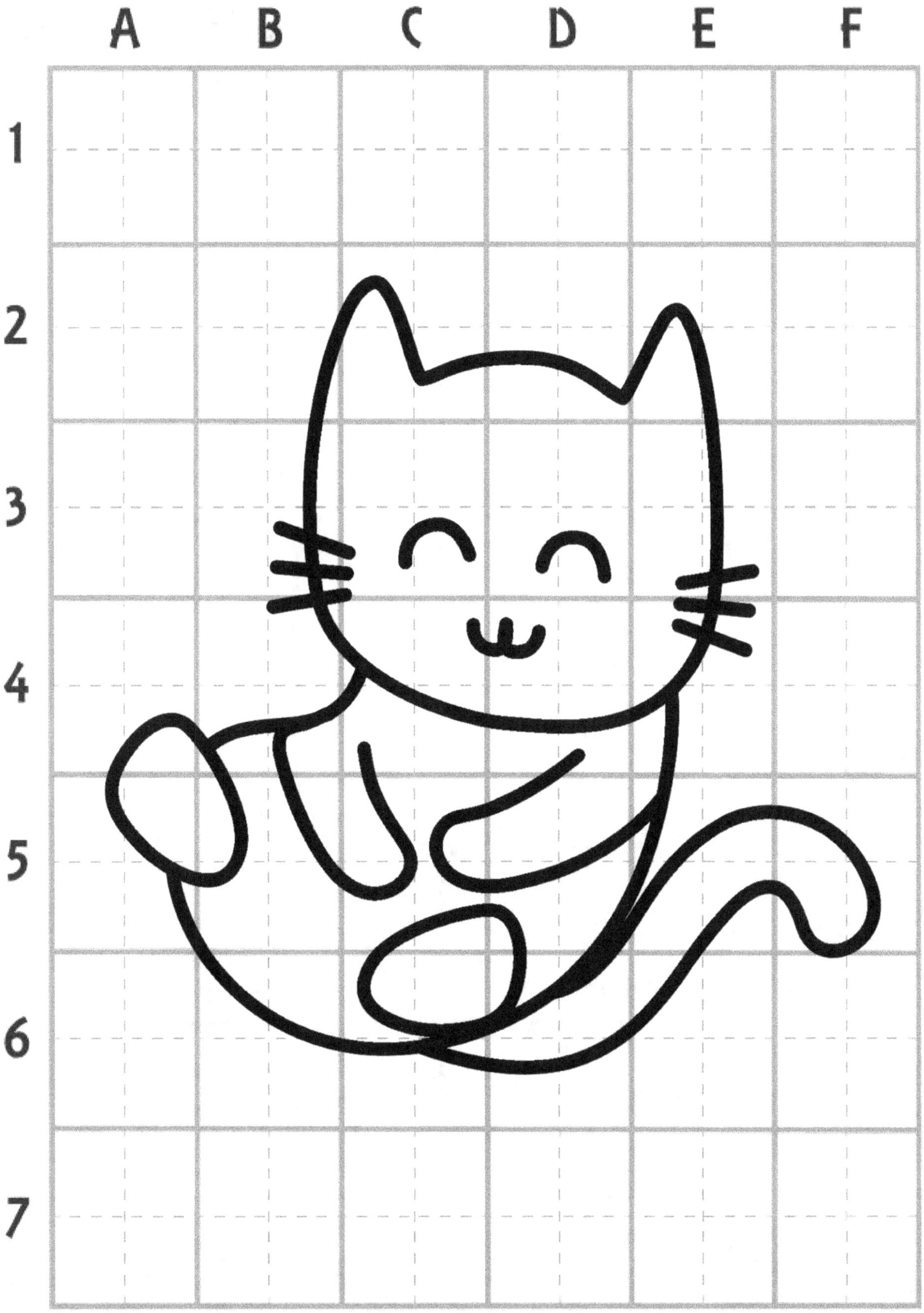
A B C D E F
1 2 3 4 5 6 7

Your Turn!

	A	B	C	D	E	F
1						
2						
3						
4						
5						
6						
7						

Practice Makes Perfect!

Draw & Color

Practice Makes Perfect!

Draw & Color

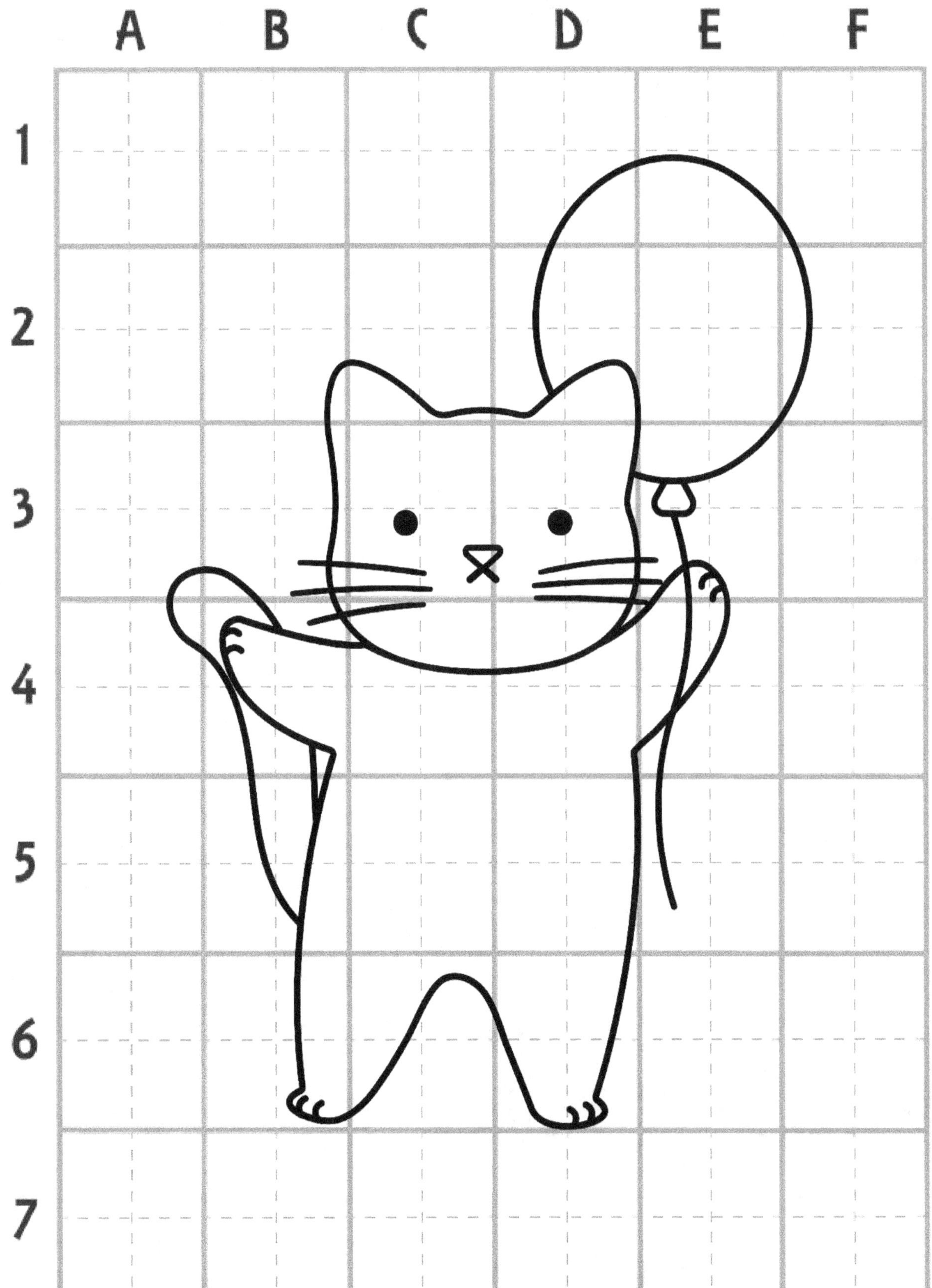
A
B
C
D
E
F
1
2
3
4
5
6
7

Your Turn!

	A	B	C	D	E	F
1						
2						
3						
4						
5						
6						
7						

Practice Makes Perfect!

Draw & Color

Practice Makes Perfect!

Draw & Color

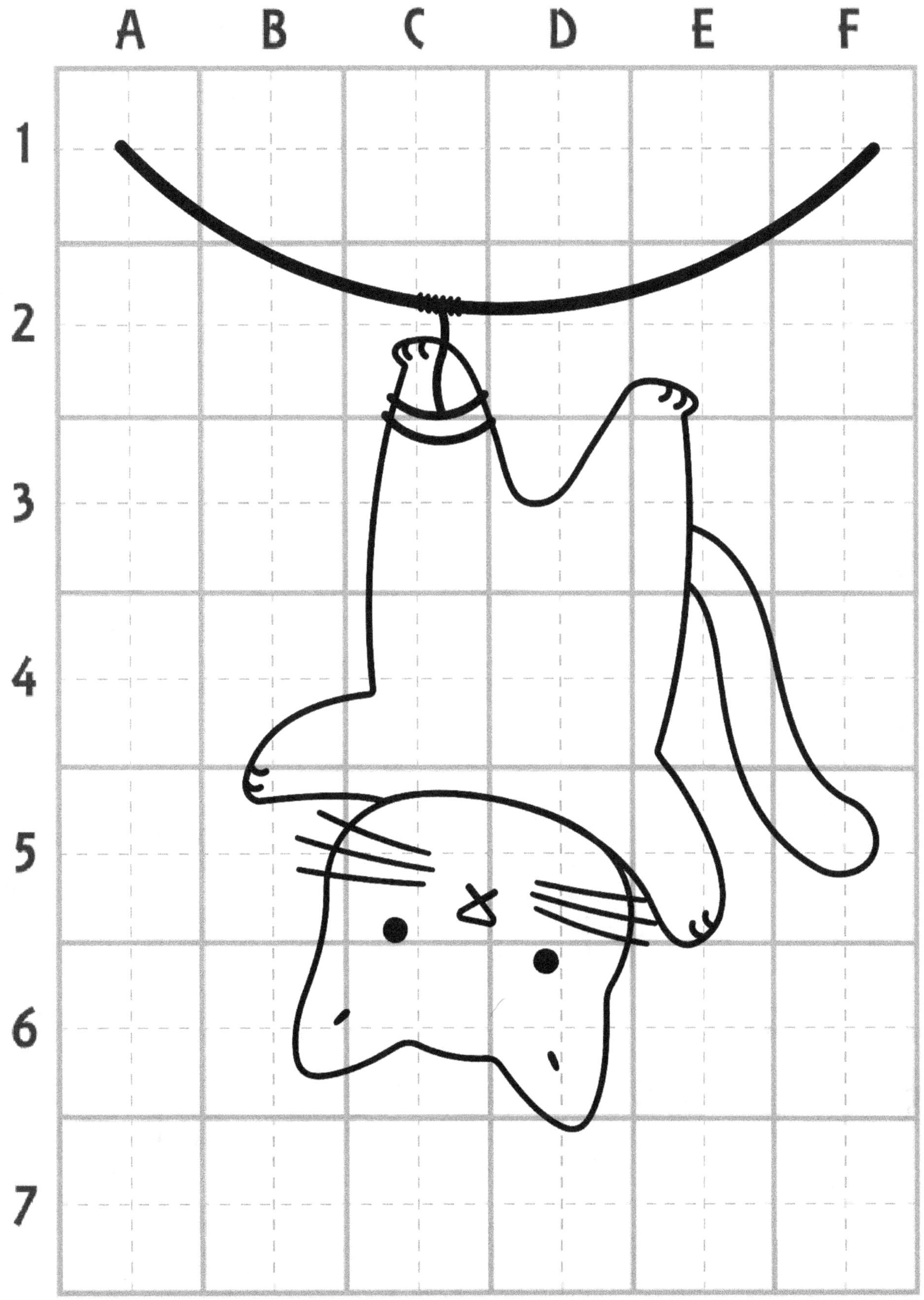
A B C D E F
1
2
3
4
5
6
7

Your Turn!

	A	B	C	D	E	F
1						
2						
3						
4						
5						
6						
7						

Practice Makes Perfect!

Draw & Color

Practice Makes Perfect!

Draw & Color

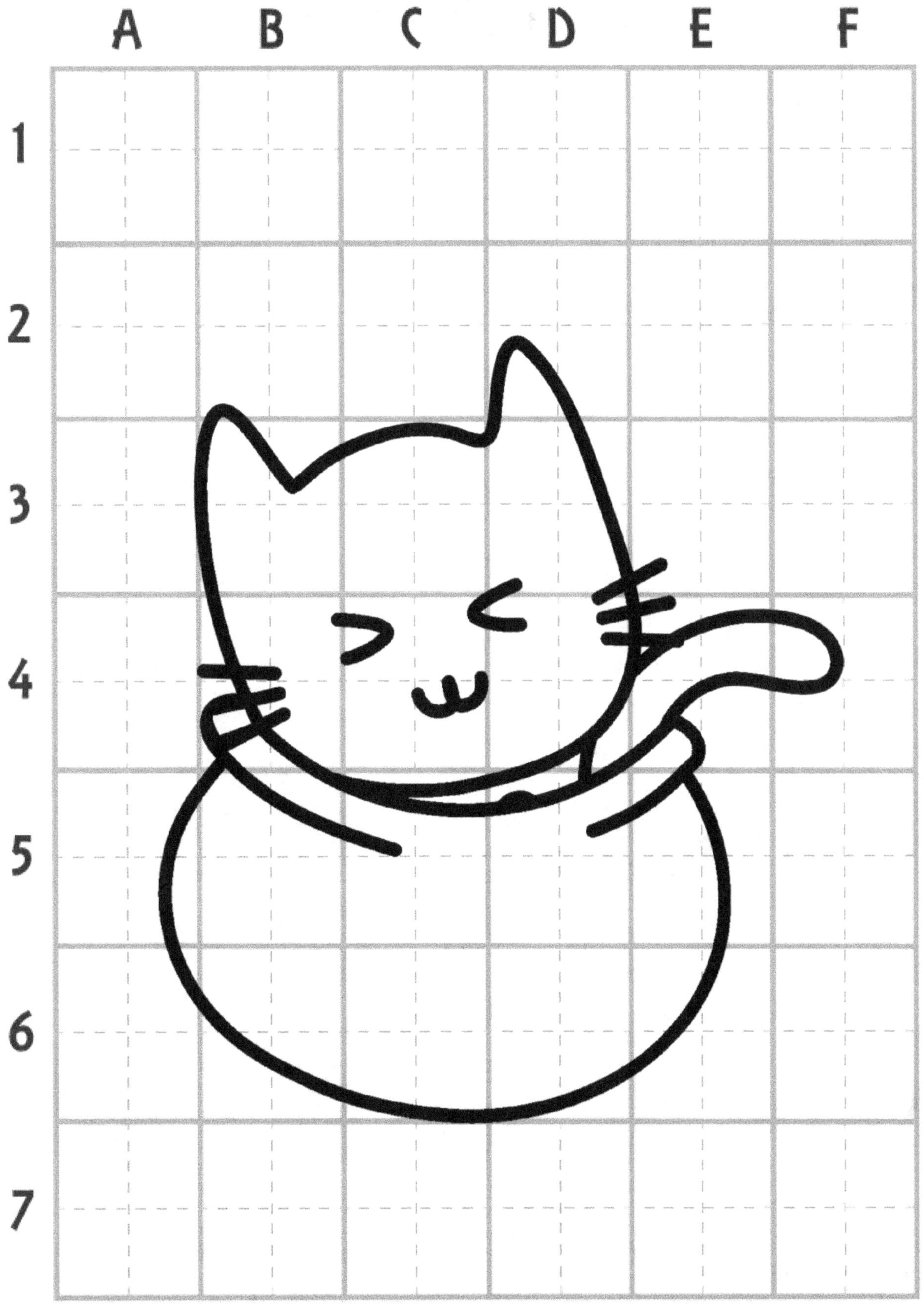
A B C D E F
1
2
3
4
5
6
7

Your Turn!

	A	B	C	D	E	F
1						
2						
3						
4						
5						
6						
7						

Practice Makes Perfect!

Draw & Color

Practice Makes Perfect!

Draw & Color

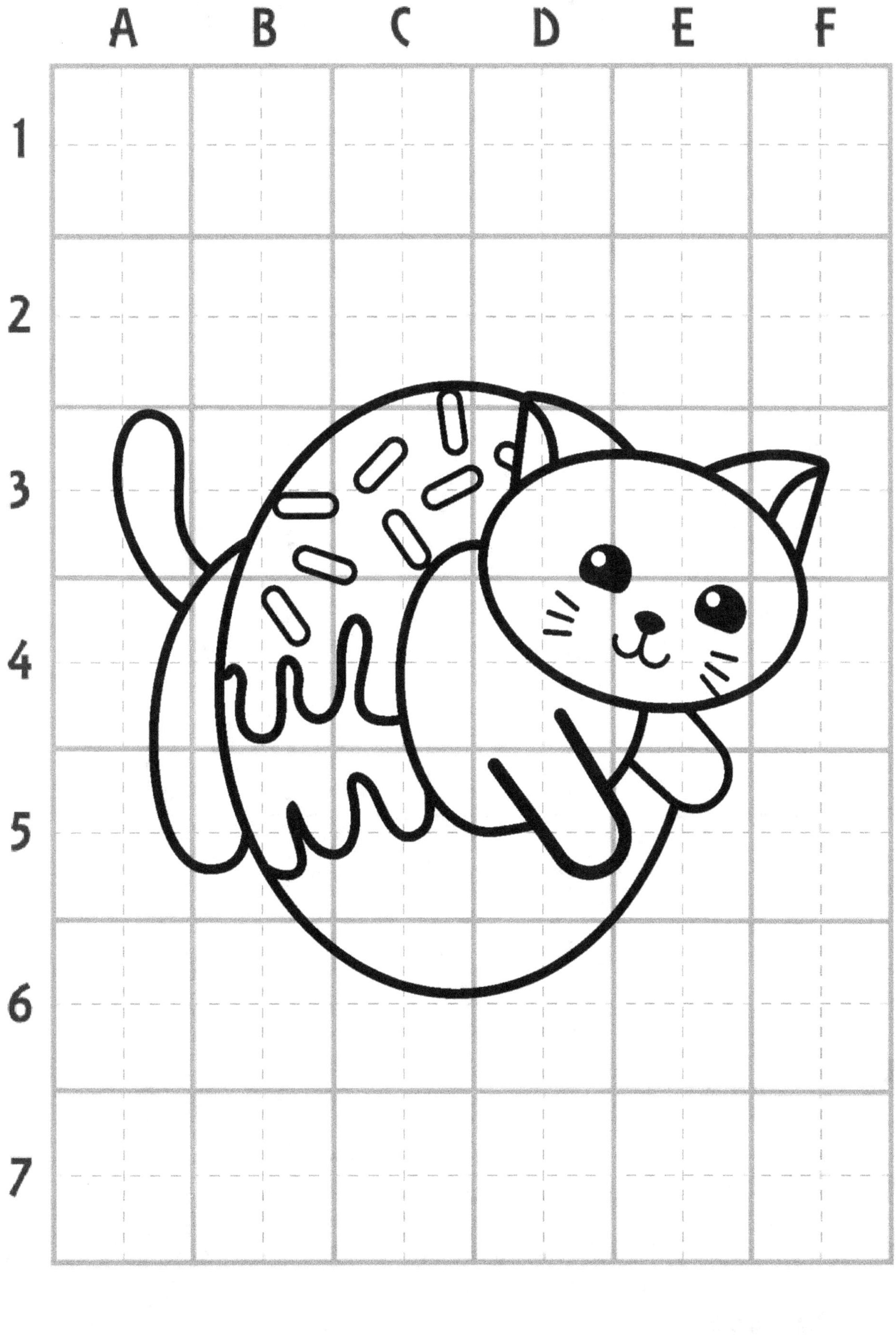
A B C D E F
1
2
3
4
5
6
7

Your Turn!

	A	B	C	D	E	F
1						
2						
3						
4						
5						
6						
7						

Practice Makes Perfect!

Draw & Color

Practice Makes Perfect!

Draw & Color

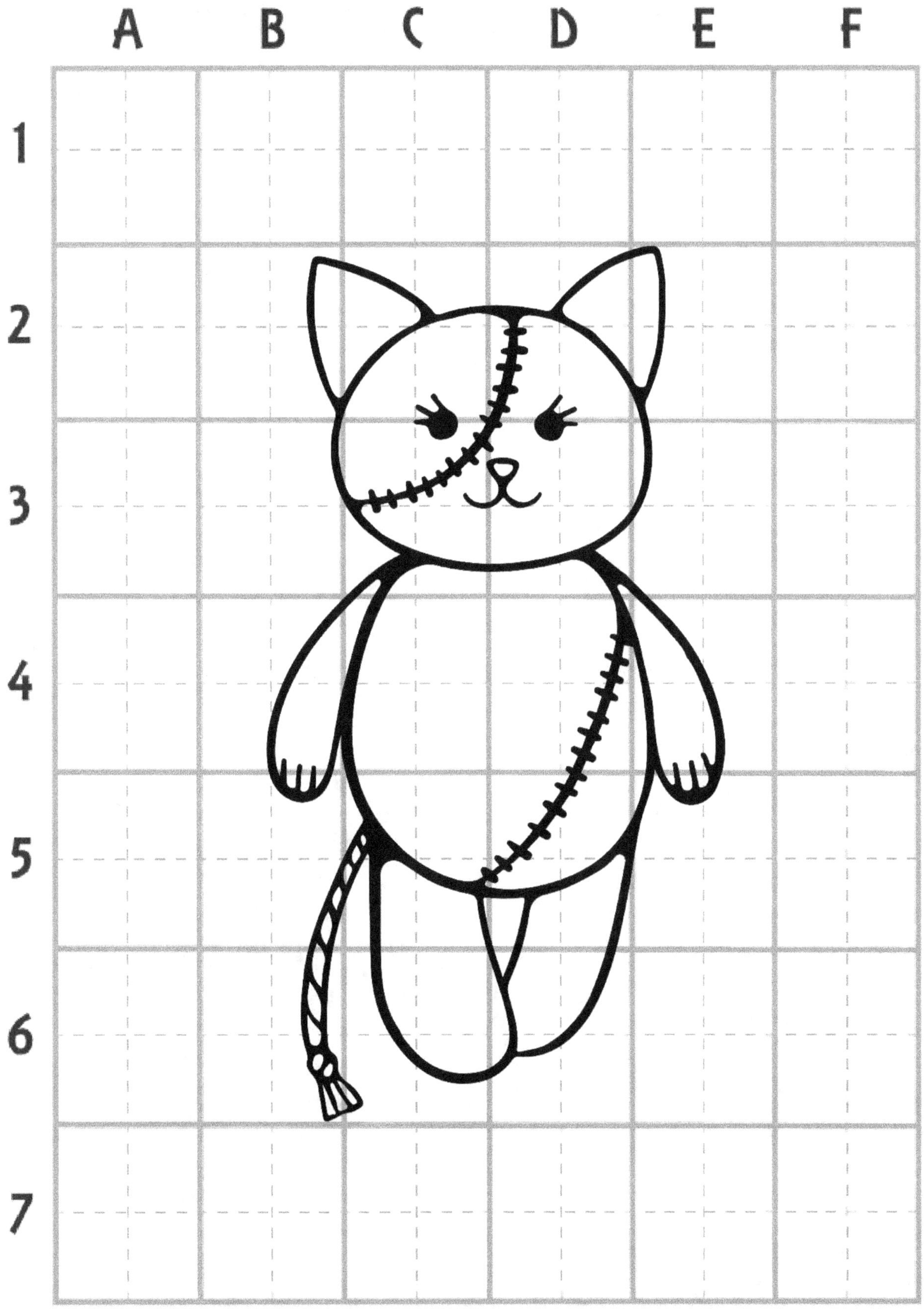
A B C D E F
1
2
3
4
5
6
7

Your Turn!

	A	B	C	D	E	F
1						
2						
3						
4						
5						
6						
7						

Practice Makes Perfect!

Draw & Color

Practice Makes Perfect!

Draw & Color

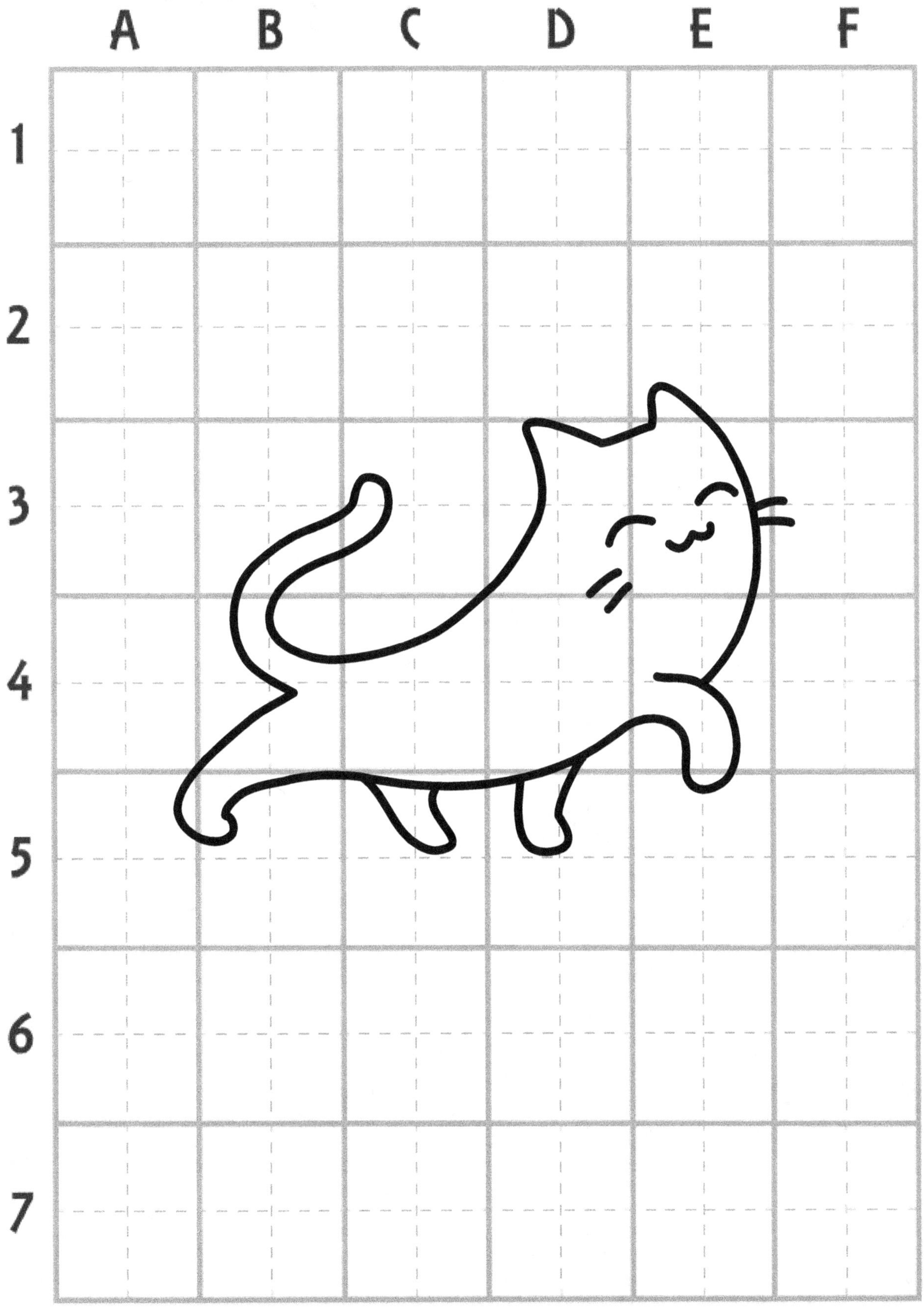

A
B
C
D
E
F
1
2
3
4
5
6
7

Your Turn!

	A	B	C	D	E	F
1						
2						
3						
4						
5						
6						
7						

Practice Makes Perfect!

Draw & Color

Practice Makes Perfect!

Draw & Color

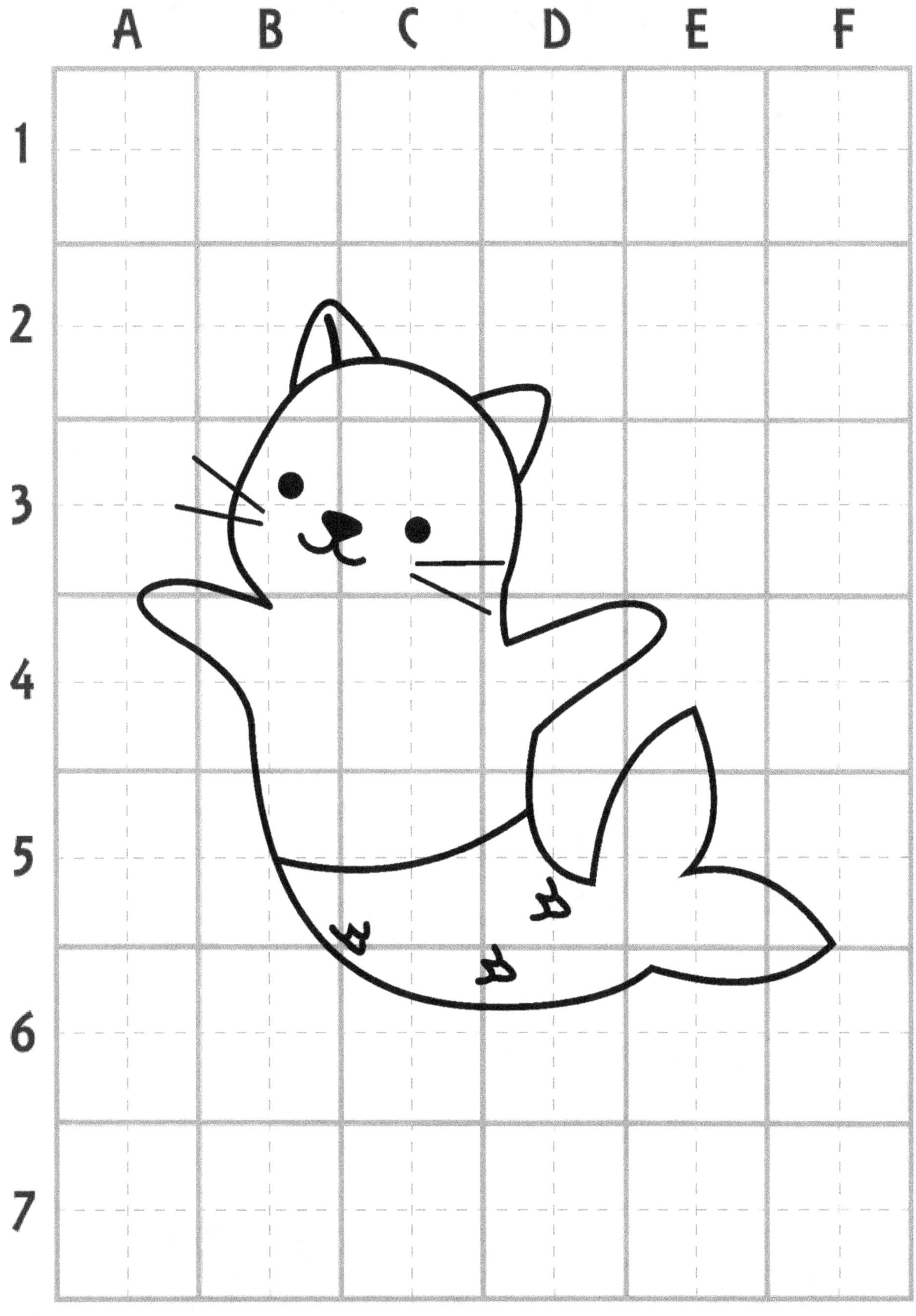
A B C D E F
1
2
3
4
5
6
7

Your Turn!

	A	B	C	D	E	F
1						
2						
3						
4						
5						
6						
7						

Practice Makes Perfect!

Draw & Color

Practice Makes Perfect!

Draw & Color

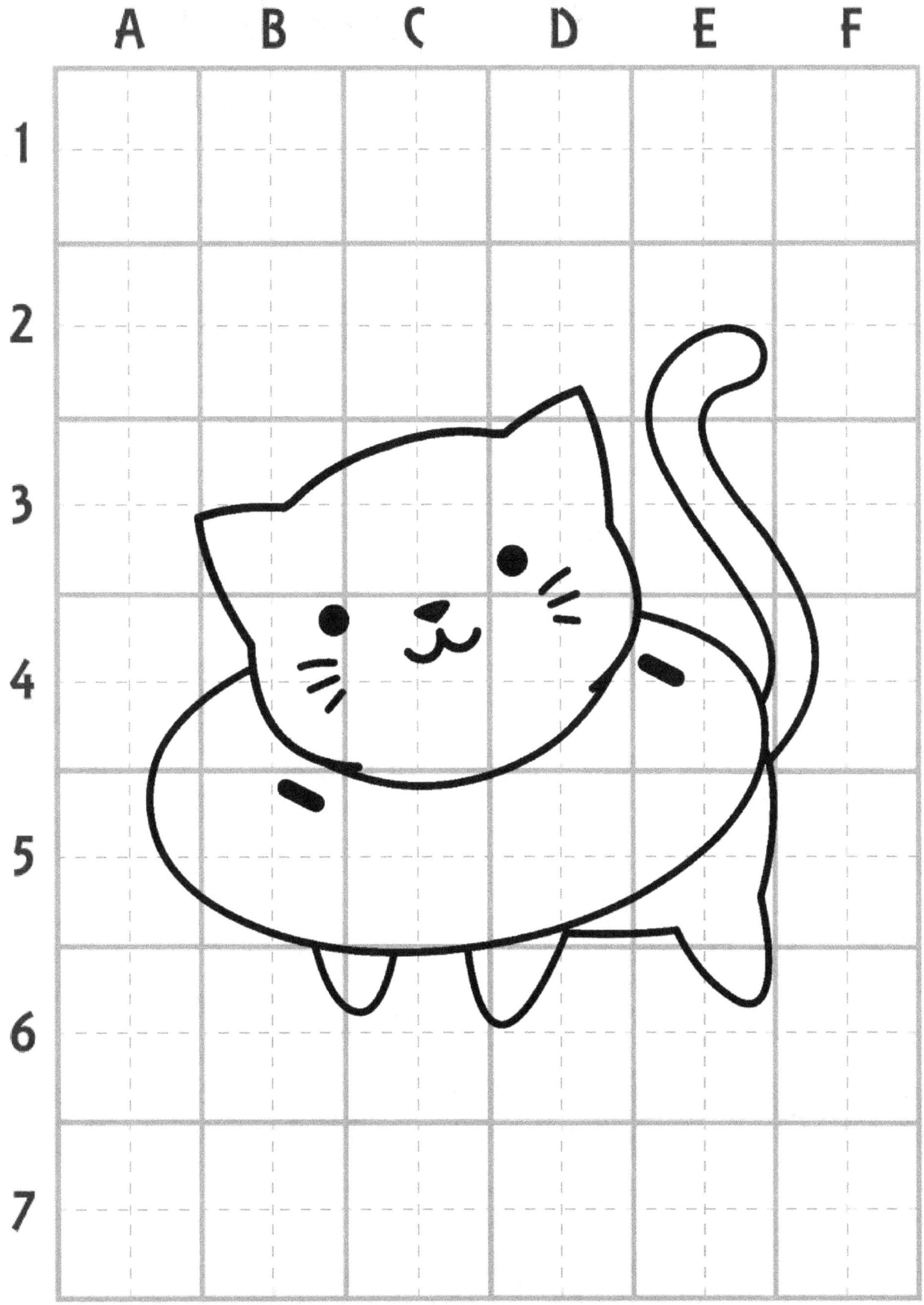
A
B
C
D
E
F
1
2
3
4
5
6
7

Your Turn!

	A	B	C	D	E	F
1						
2						
3						
4						
5						
6						
7						

Practice Makes Perfect!

Draw & Color

Practice Makes Perfect!

Draw & Color

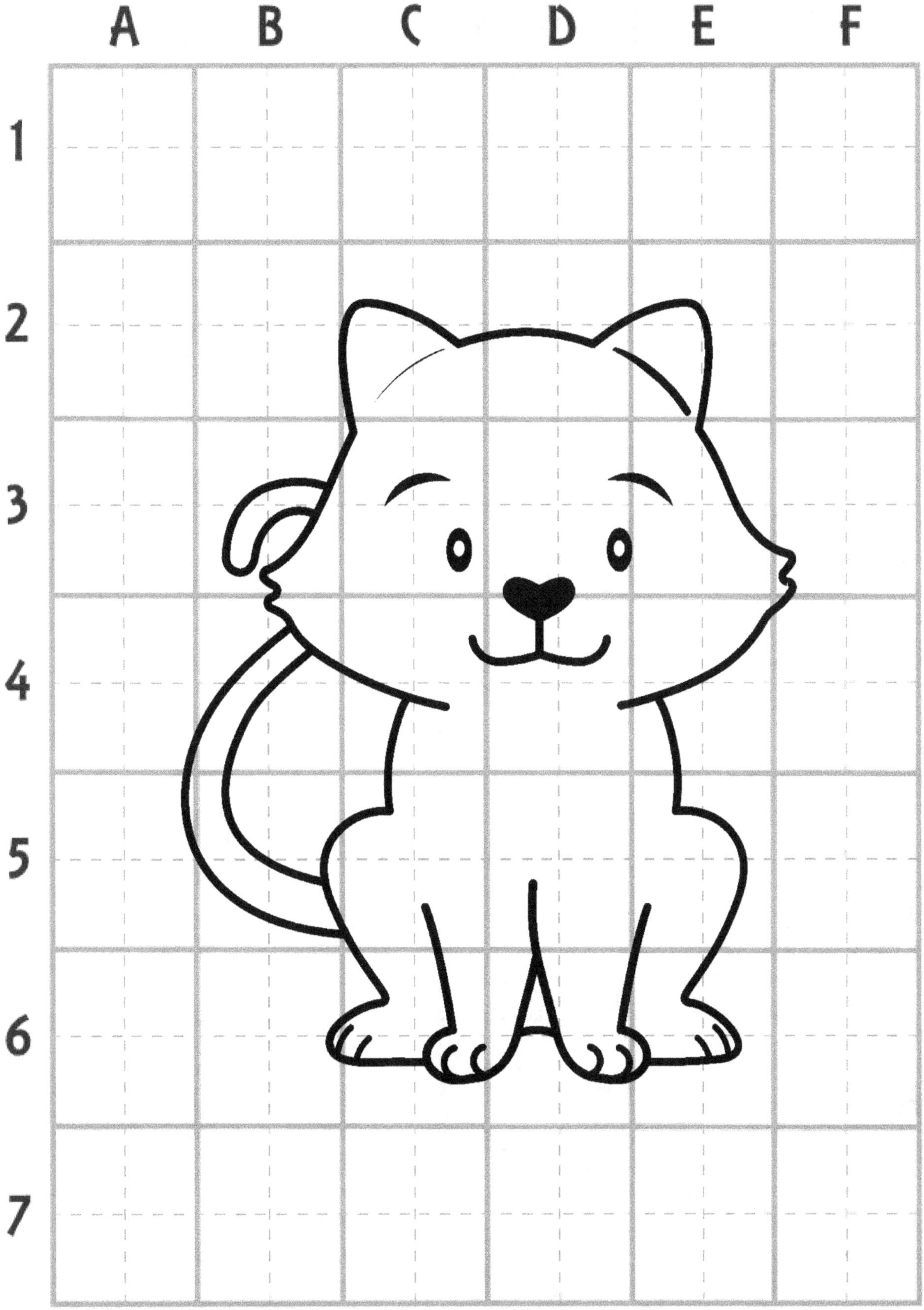
A
B
C
D
E
F
1
2
3
4
5
6
7

Your Turn!

	A	B	C	D	E	F
1						
2						
3						
4						
5						
6						
7						

Practice Makes Perfect!

Draw & Color

Practice Makes Perfect!

Draw & Color

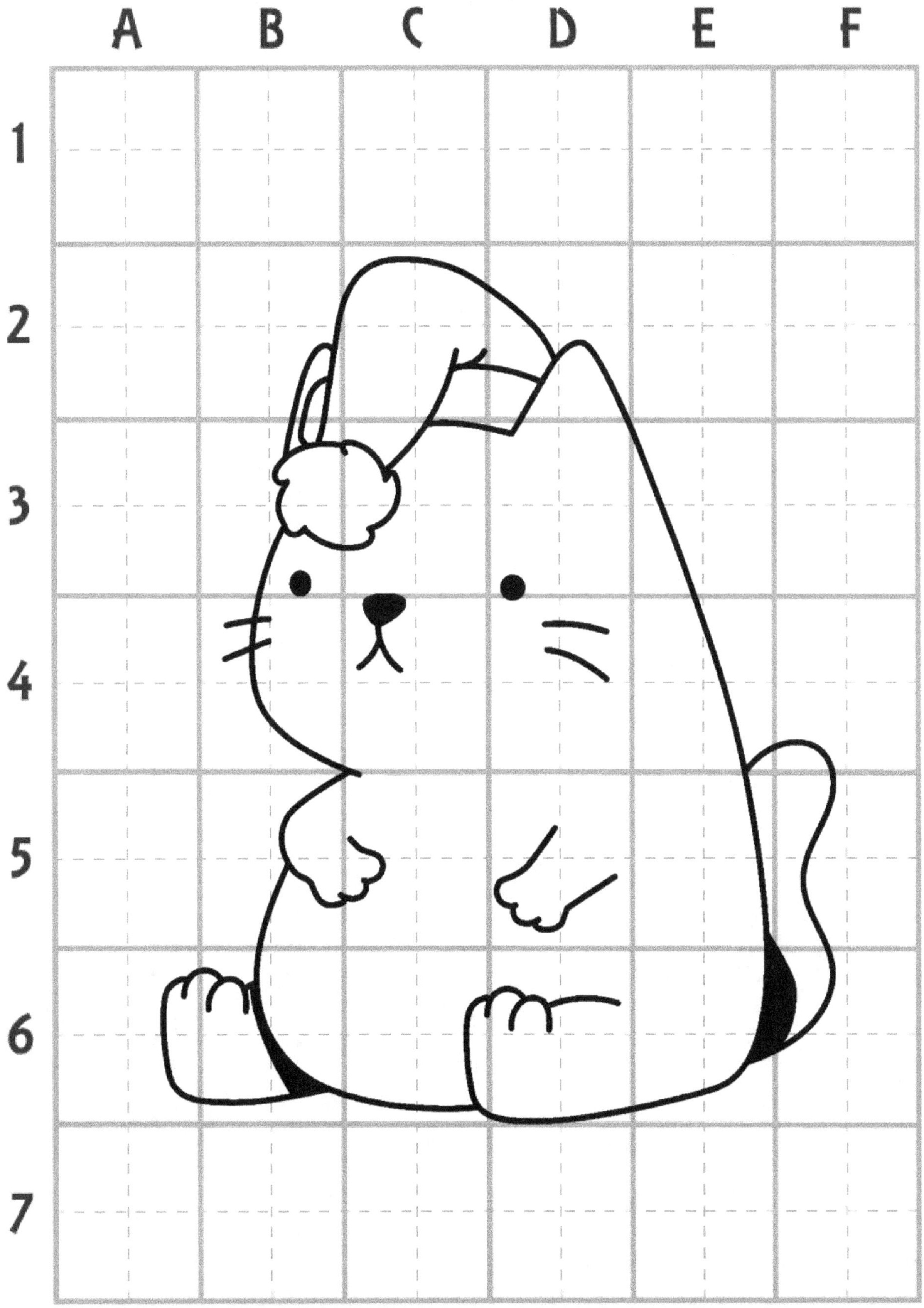
A B C D E F
1 2 3 4 5 6 7

Your Turn!

	A	B	C	D	E	F
1						
2						
3						
4						
5						
6						
7						

Practice Makes Perfect!

Draw & Color

Practice Makes Perfect!

Draw & Color

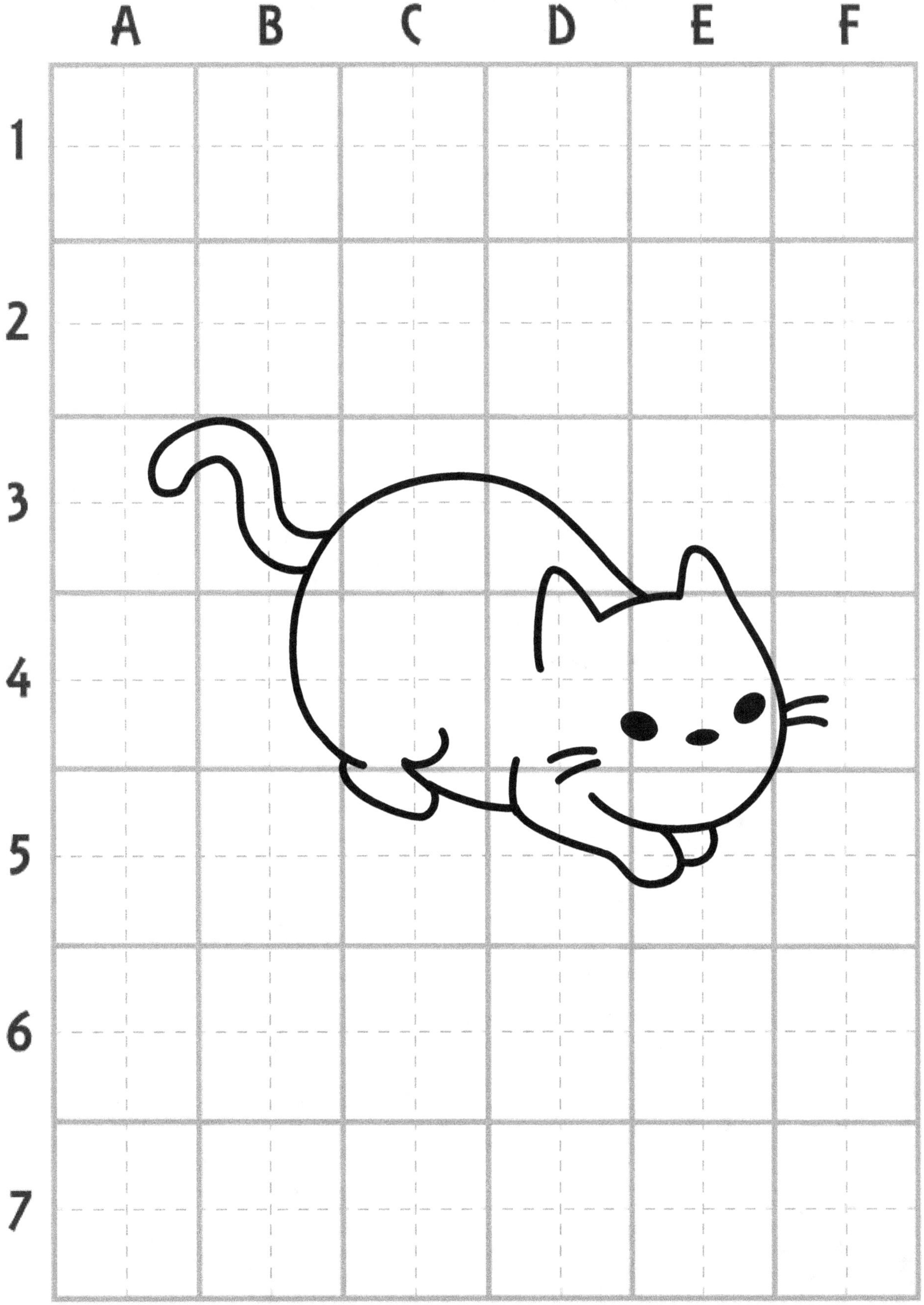
A B C D E F
1
2
3
4
5
6
7

Your Turn!

	A	B	C	D	E	F
1						
2						
3						
4						
5						
6						
7						

Practice Makes Perfect!

Draw & Color

Practice Makes Perfect!

Draw & Color

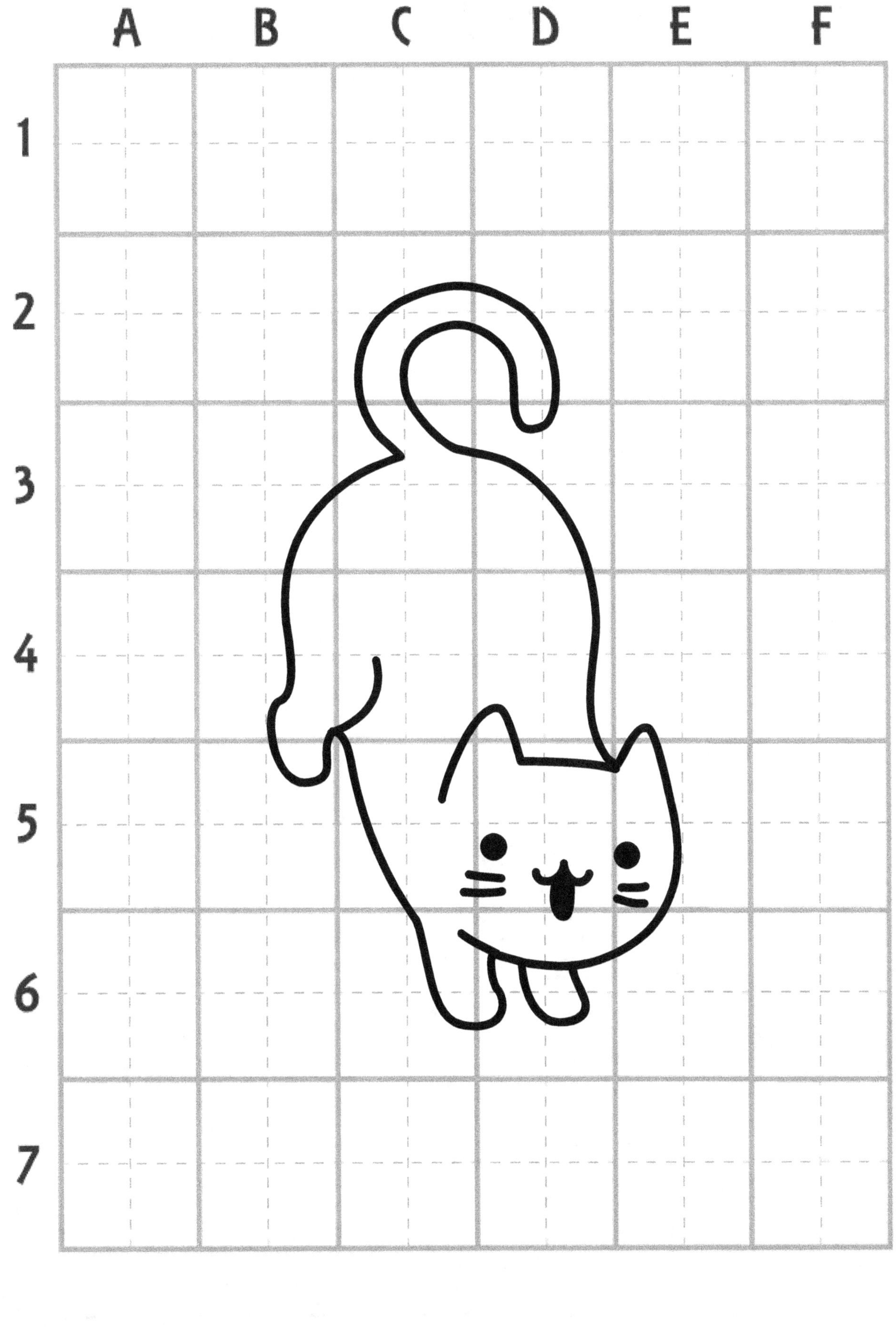
A B C D E F
1
2
3
4
5
6
7

Your Turn!

	A	B	C	D	E	F
1						
2						
3						
4						
5						
6						
7						

Practice Makes Perfect!

Draw & Color

Practice Makes Perfect!

Draw & Color

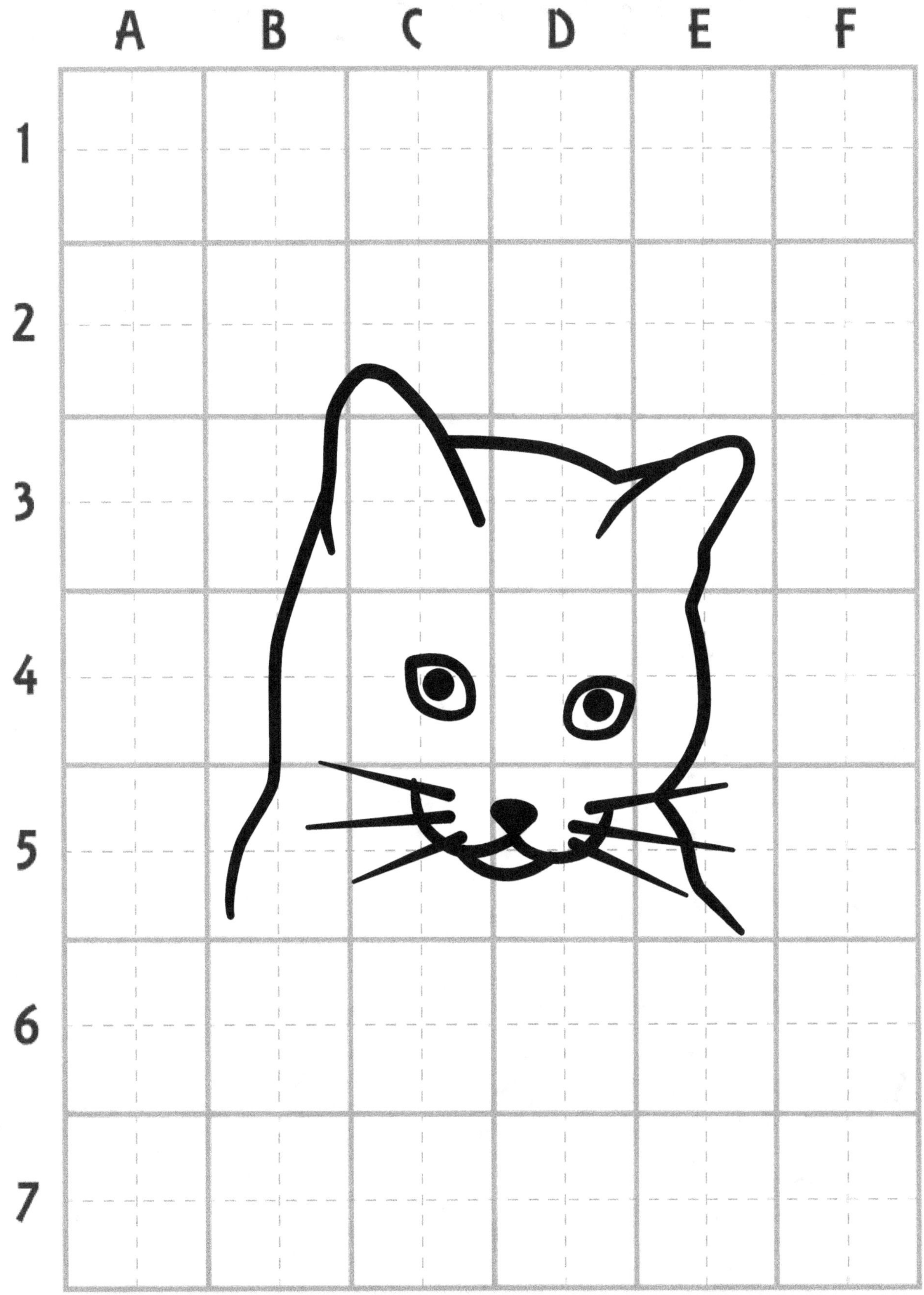
A
B
C
D
E
F
1
2
3
4
5
6
7

Your Turn!

	A	B	C	D	E	F
1						
2						
3						
4						
5						
6						
7						

Practice Makes Perfect!

Draw & Color

Practice Makes Perfect!

Draw & Color

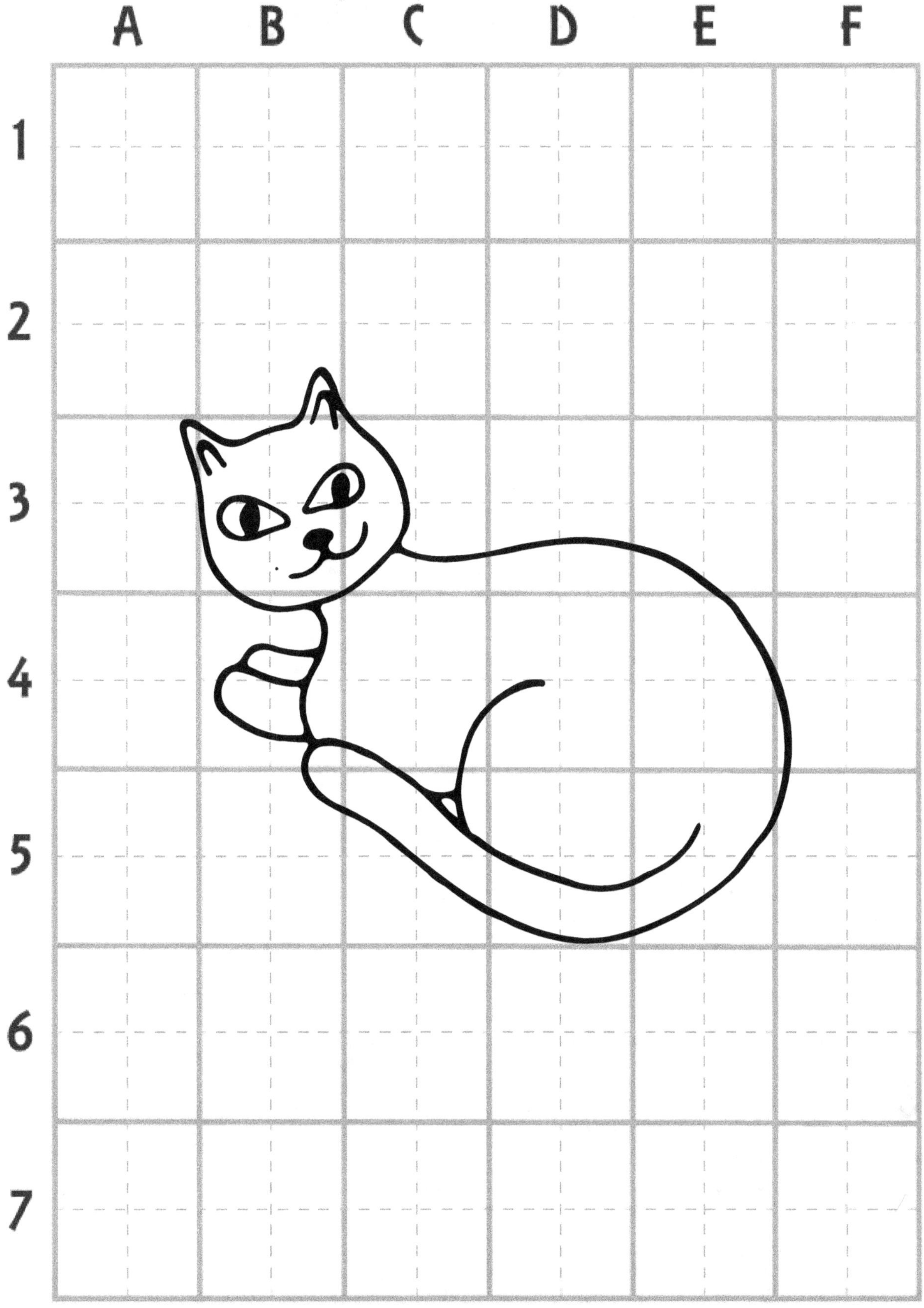
A B C D E F
1 2 3 4 5 6 7

Your Turn!

	A	B	C	D	E	F
1						
2						
3						
4						
5						
6						
7						

Practice Makes Perfect!

Draw & Color

Practice Makes Perfect!

Draw & Color

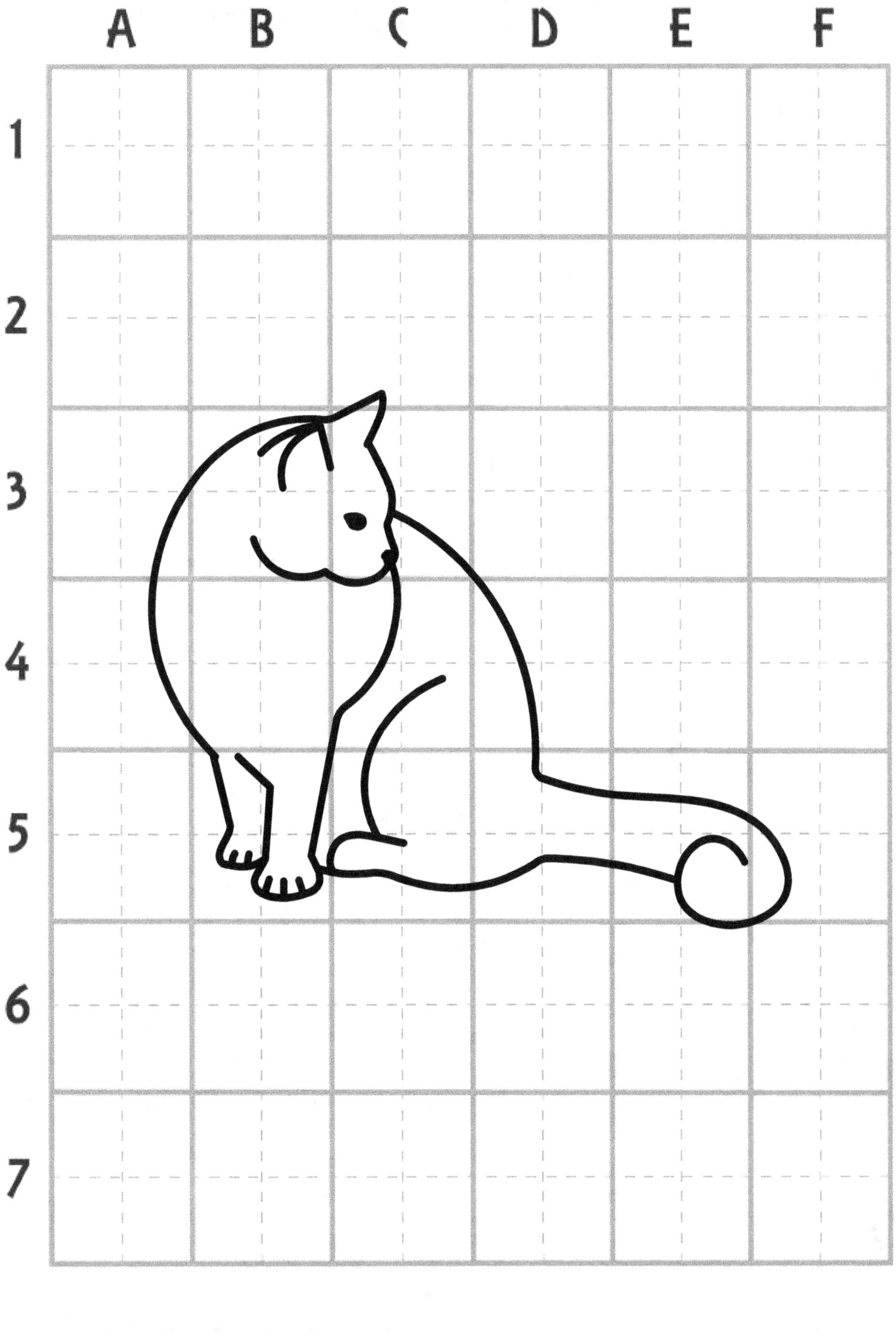
A
B
C
D
E
F
1
2
3
4
5
6
7

Your Turn!

	A	B	C	D	E	F
1						
2						
3						
4						
5						
6						
7						

Practice Makes Perfect!

Draw & Color

Practice Makes Perfect!

Draw & Color

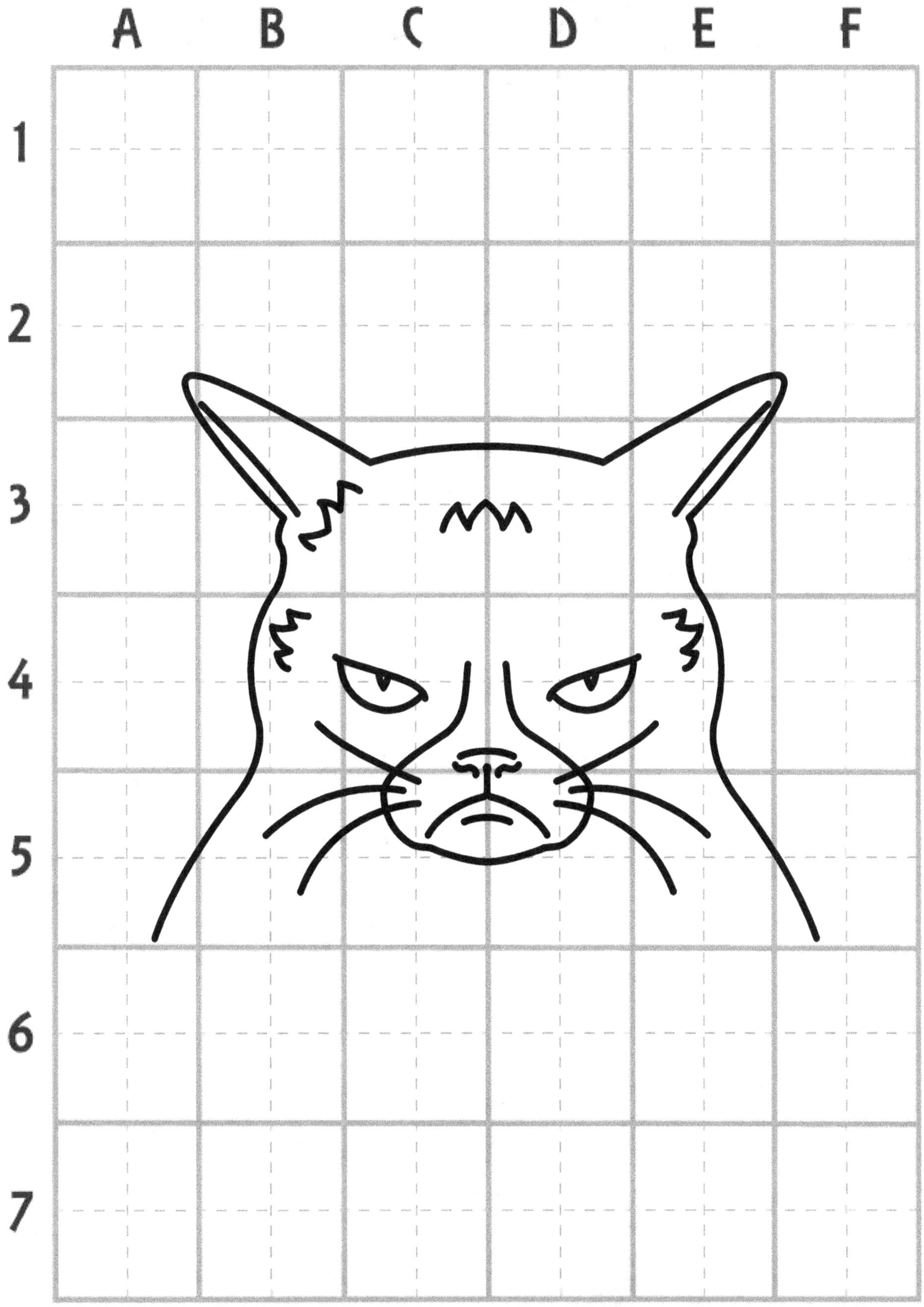
A
B
C
D
E
F
1
2
3
4
5
6
7

Your Turn!

	A	B	C	D	E	F
1						
2						
3						
4						
5						
6						
7						

Practice Makes Perfect!

Draw & Color

Practice Makes Perfect!

Draw & Color

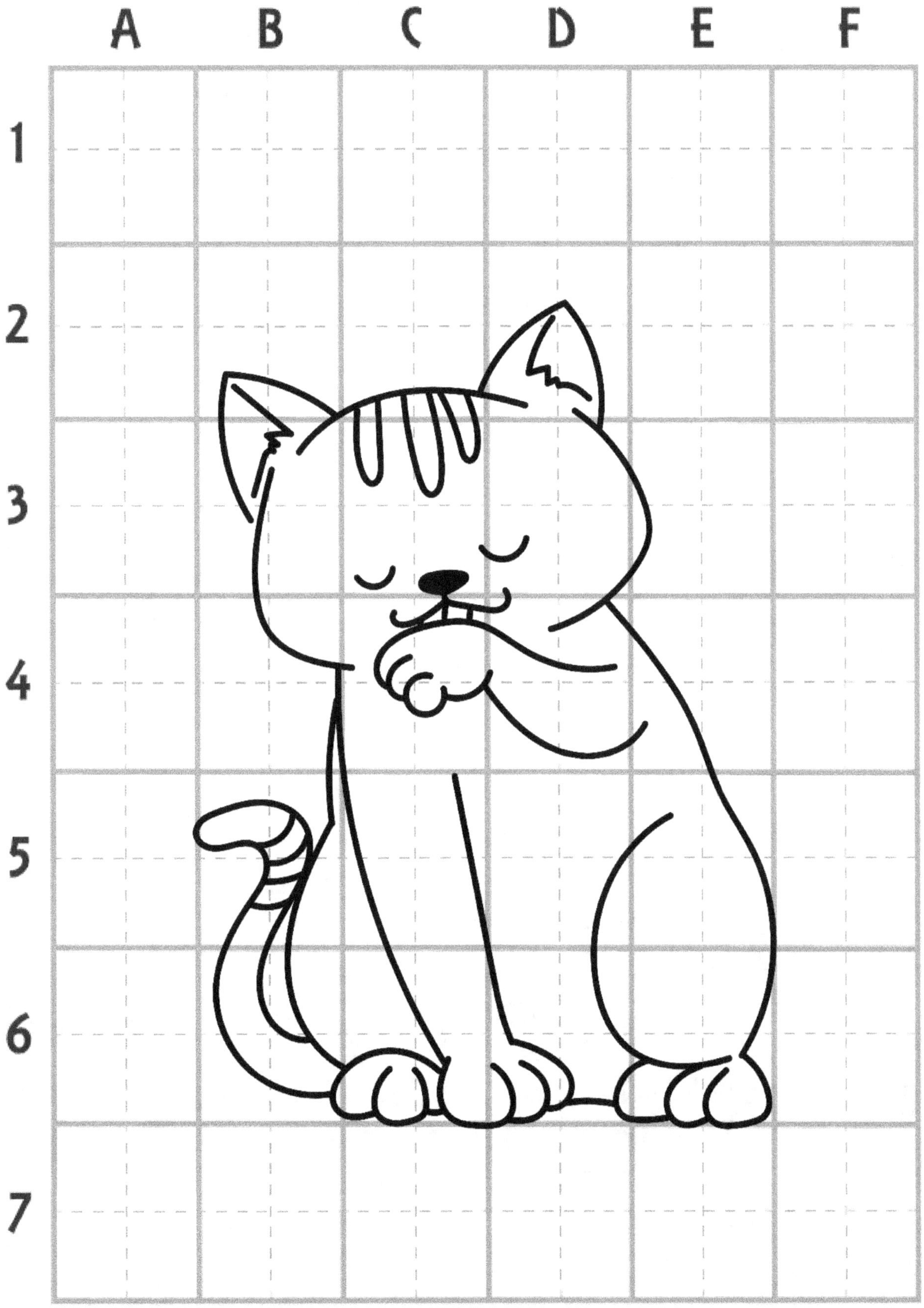
A B C D E F
1 2 3 4 5 6 7

Your Turn!

	A	B	C	D	E	F
1						
2						
3						
4						
5						
6						
7						

Practice Makes Perfect!

Draw & Color

Practice Makes Perfect!

Draw & Color

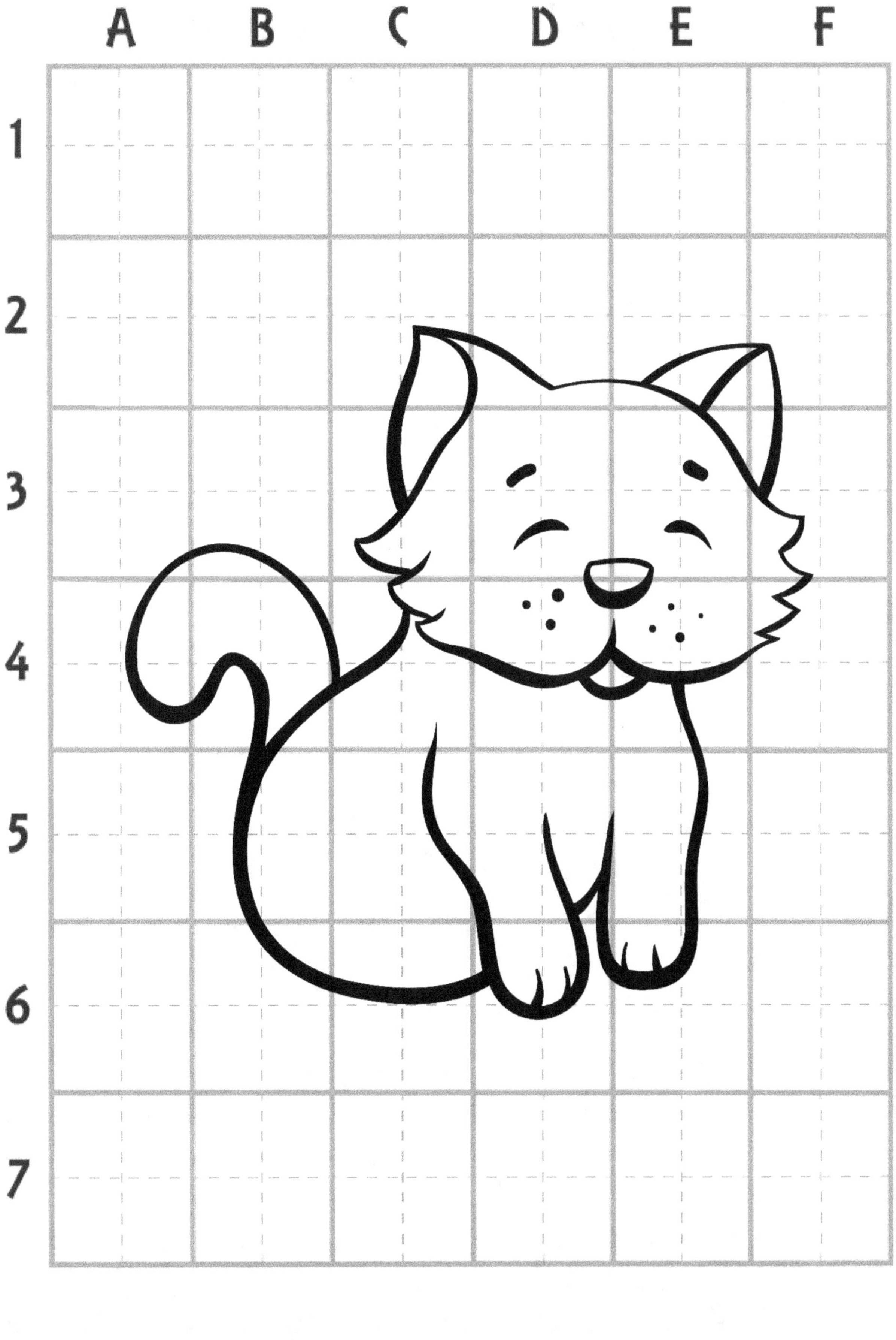
A
B
C
D
E
F
1
2
3
4
5
6
7

Your Turn!

	A	B	C	D	E	F
1						
2						
3						
4						
5						
6						
7						

Practice Makes Perfect!

Draw & Color

Practice Makes Perfect!

Draw & Color

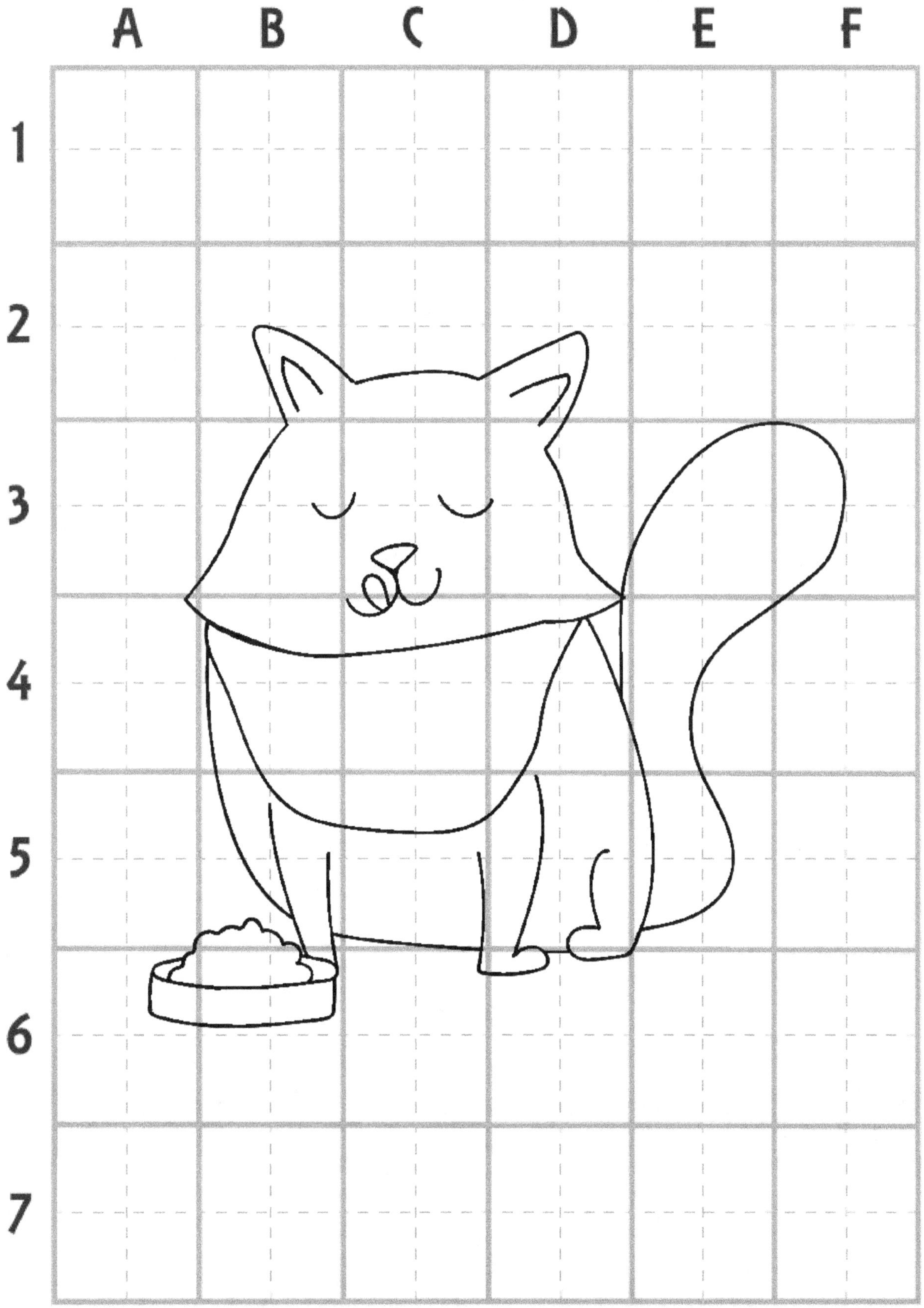
A
B
C
D
E
F
1
2
3
4
5
6
7

Your Turn!

	A	B	C	D	E	F
1						
2						
3						
4						
5						
6						
7						

Practice Makes Perfect!

Draw & Color

Practice Makes Perfect!

Draw & Color

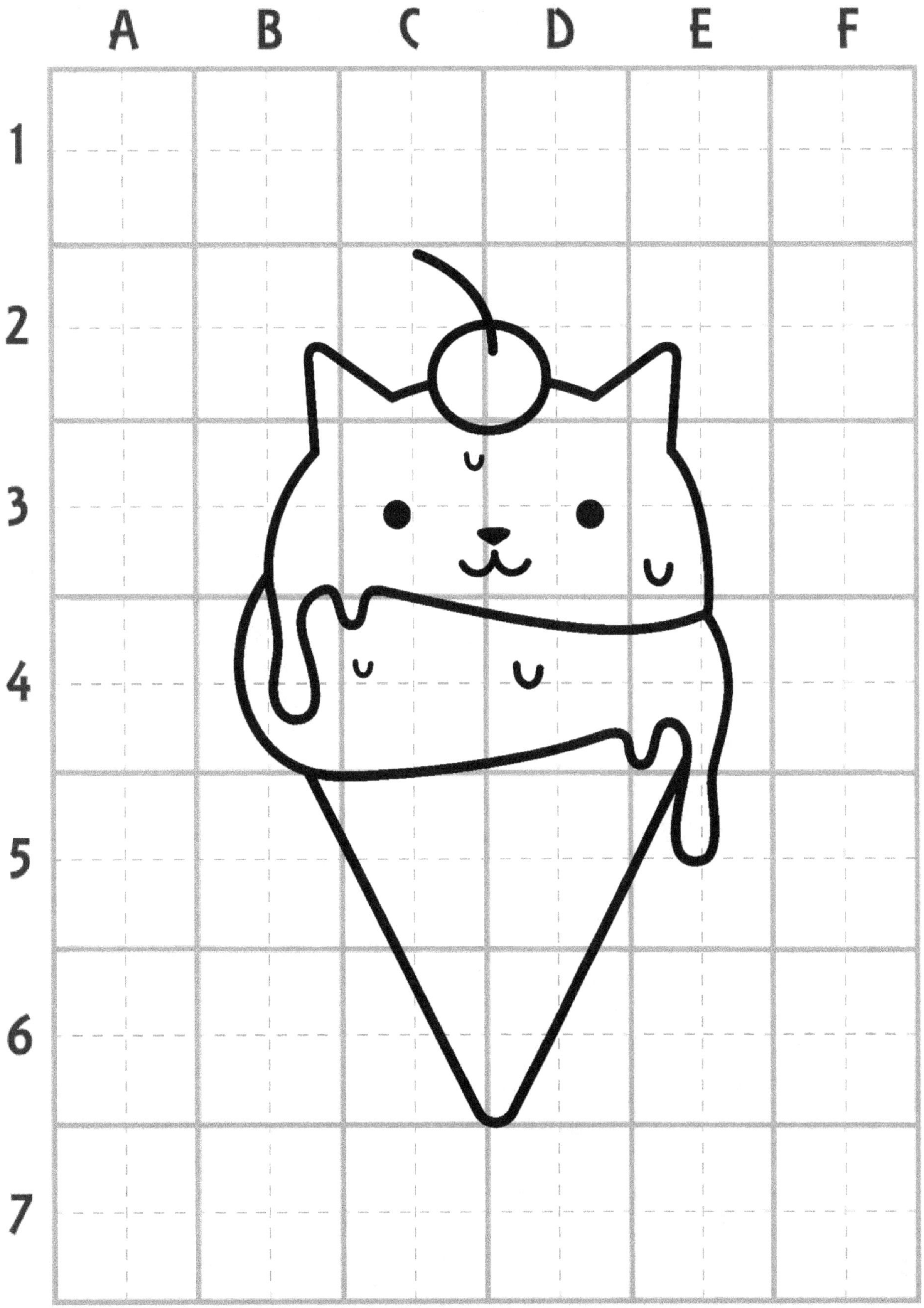

Your Turn!

	A	B	C	D	E	F
1						
2						
3						
4						
5						
6						
7						

Practice Makes Perfect!

Draw & Color

Practice Makes Perfect!

Draw & Color

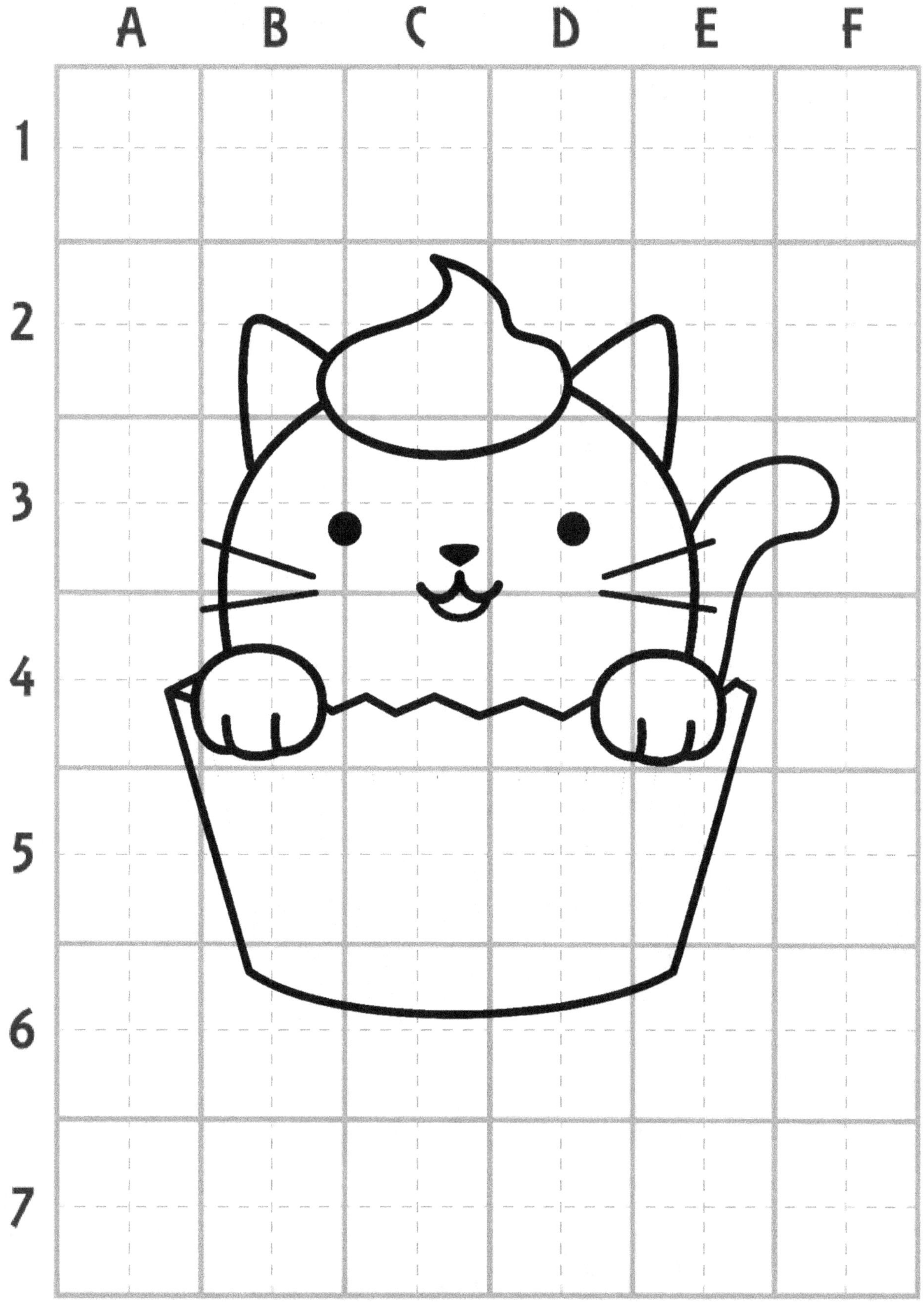
A B C D E F
1 2 3 4 5 6 7

Your Turn!

	A	B	C	D	E	F
1						
2						
3						
4						
5						
6						
7						

Practice Makes Perfect!

Draw & Color

Practice Makes Perfect!

Draw & Color

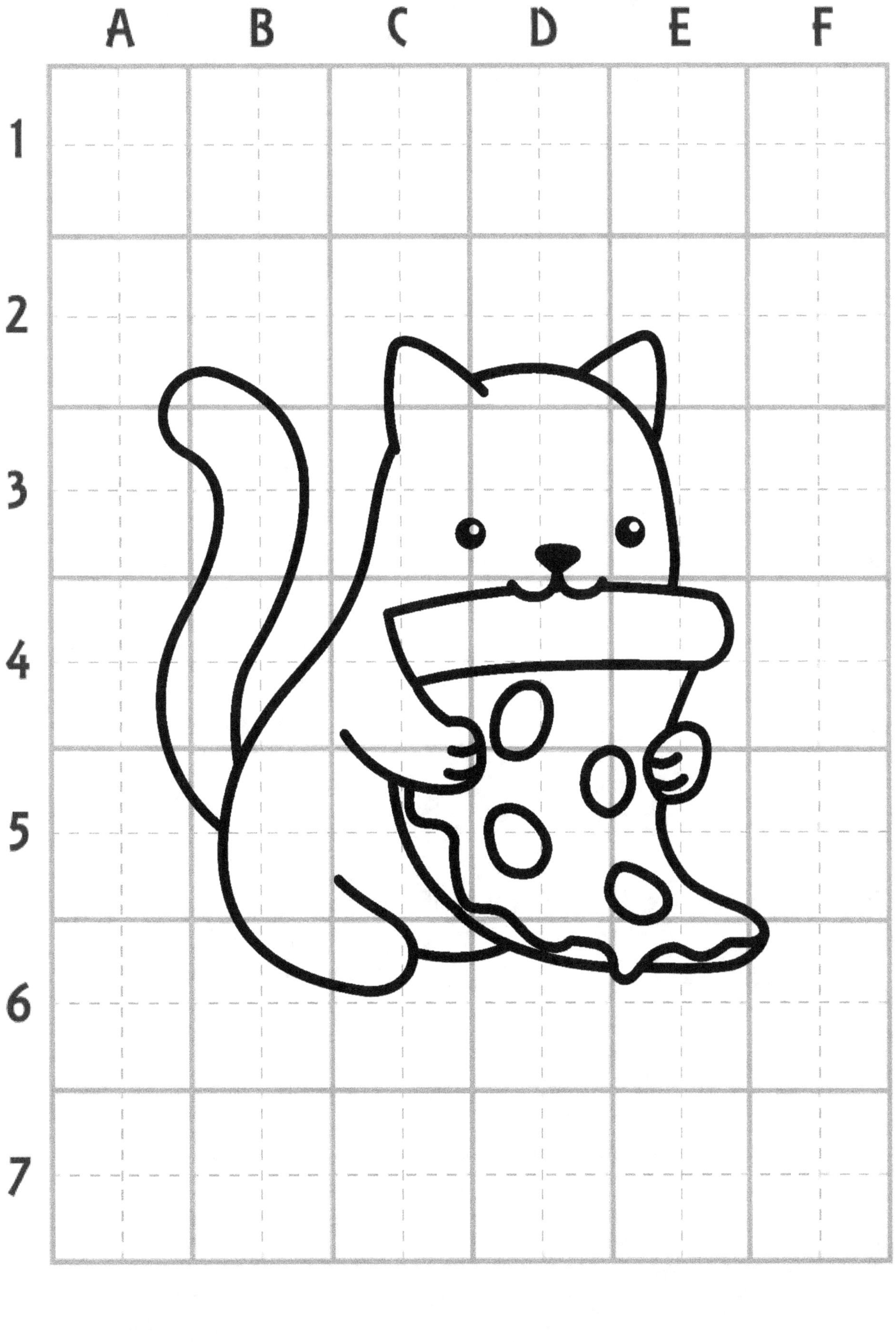
A B C D E F
1
2
3
4
5
6
7

Your Turn!

	A	B	C	D	E	F
1						
2						
3						
4						
5						
6						
7						

Practice Makes Perfect!

Draw & Color

Practice Makes Perfect!

Draw & Color

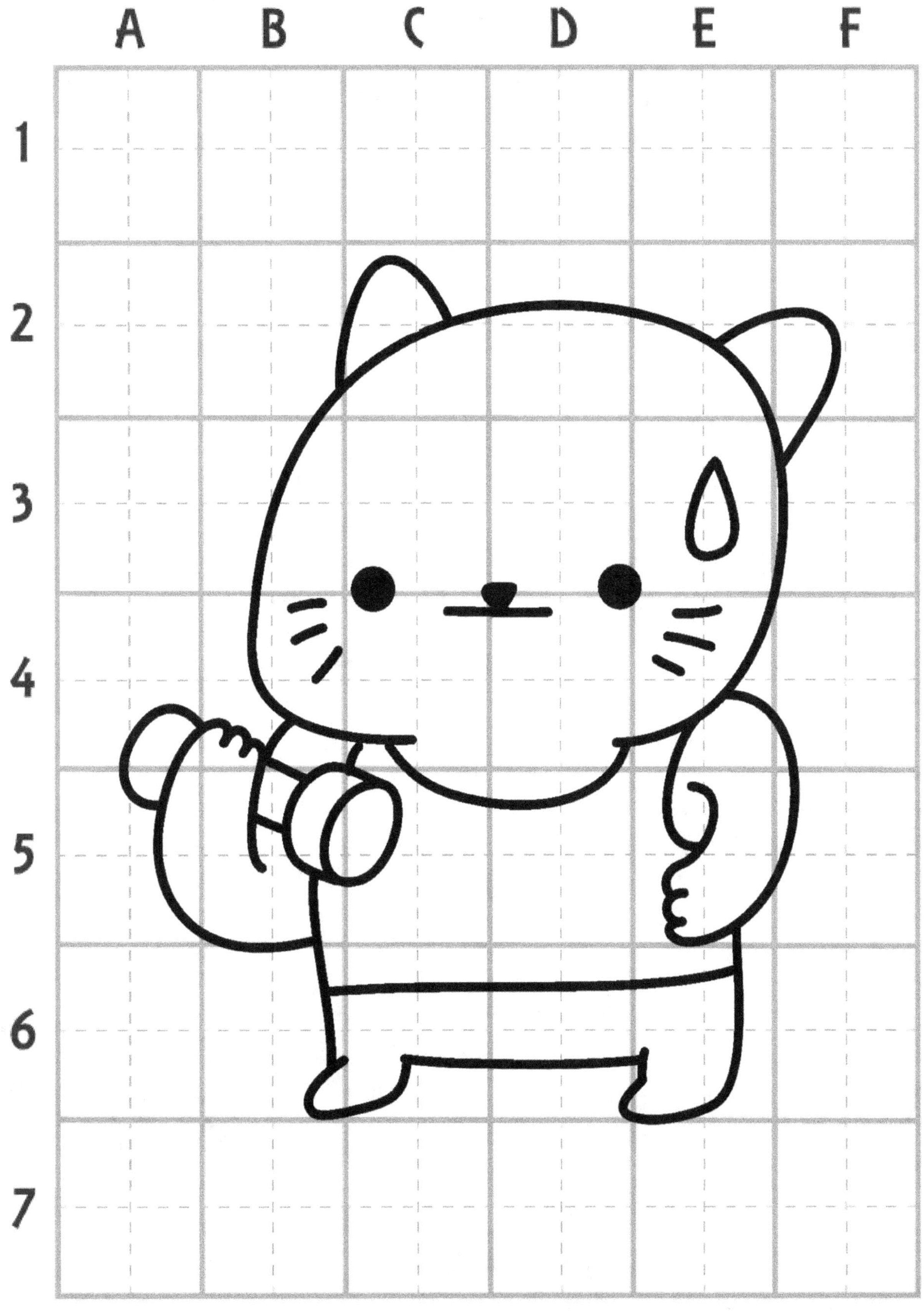
A
B
C
D
E
F
1
2
3
4
5
6
7

Your Turn!

	A	B	C	D	E	F
1						
2						
3						
4						
5						
6						
7						

Practice Makes Perfect!

Draw & Color

Practice Makes Perfect!

Draw & Color

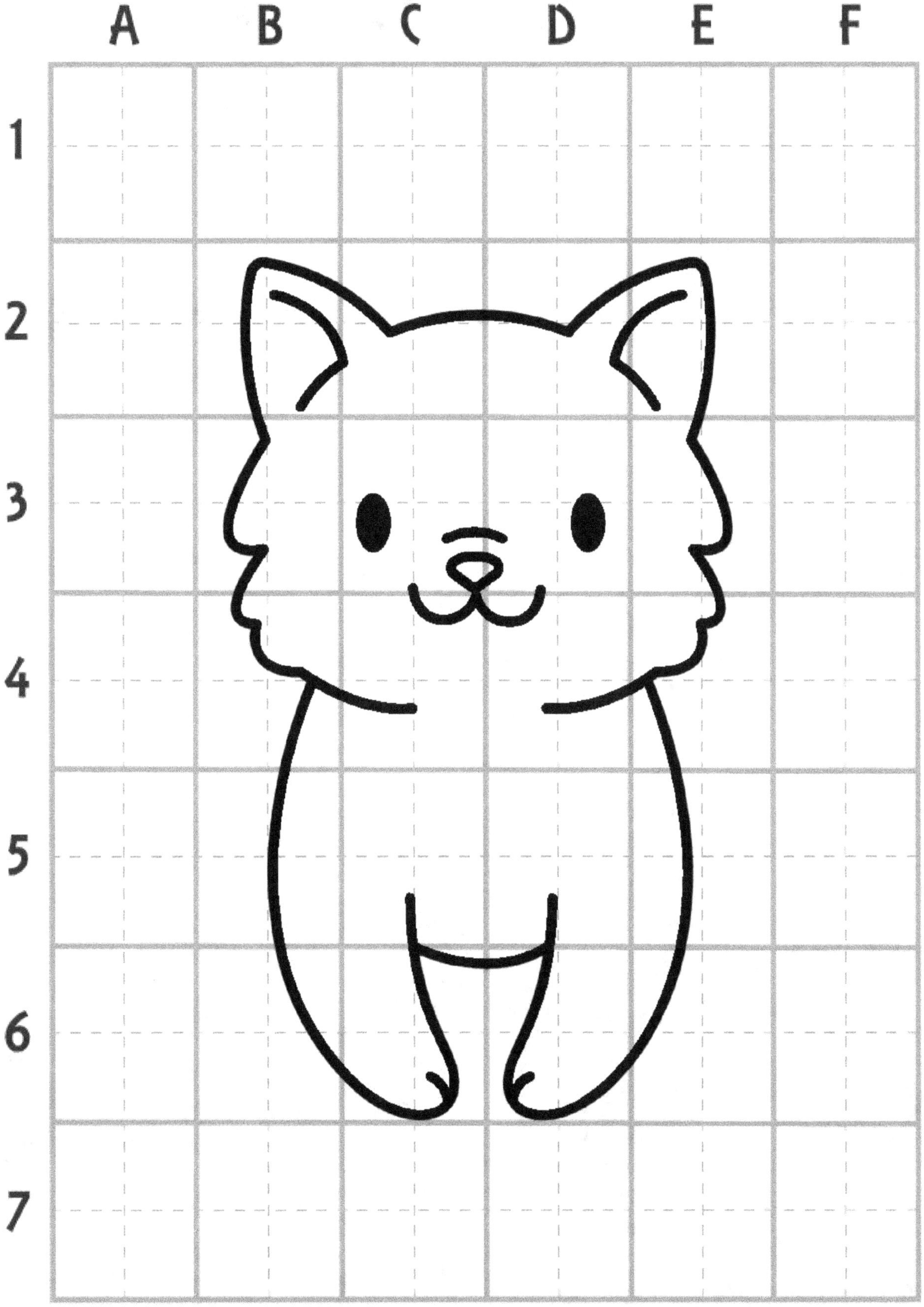
A B C D E F
1 2 3 4 5 6 7

Your Turn!

	A	B	C	D	E	F
1						
2						
3						
4						
5						
6						
7						

Practice Makes Perfect!

Draw & Color

Practice Makes Perfect!

Draw & Color

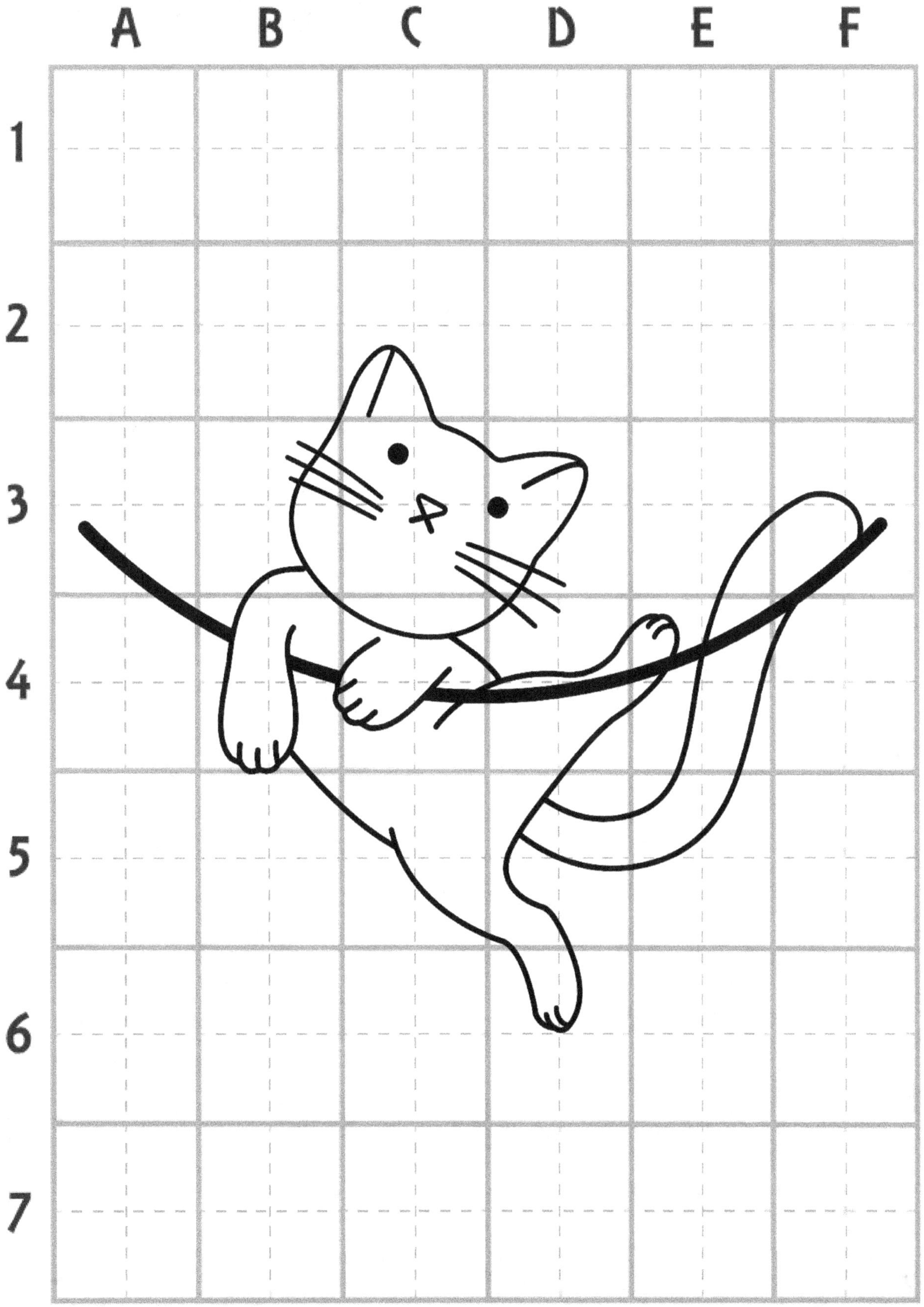
A
B
C
D
E
F
1
2
3
4
5
6
7

Your Turn!

	A	B	C	D	E	F
1						
2						
3						
4						
5						
6						
7						

Practice Makes Perfect!

Draw & Color

Practice Makes Perfect!

Draw & Color

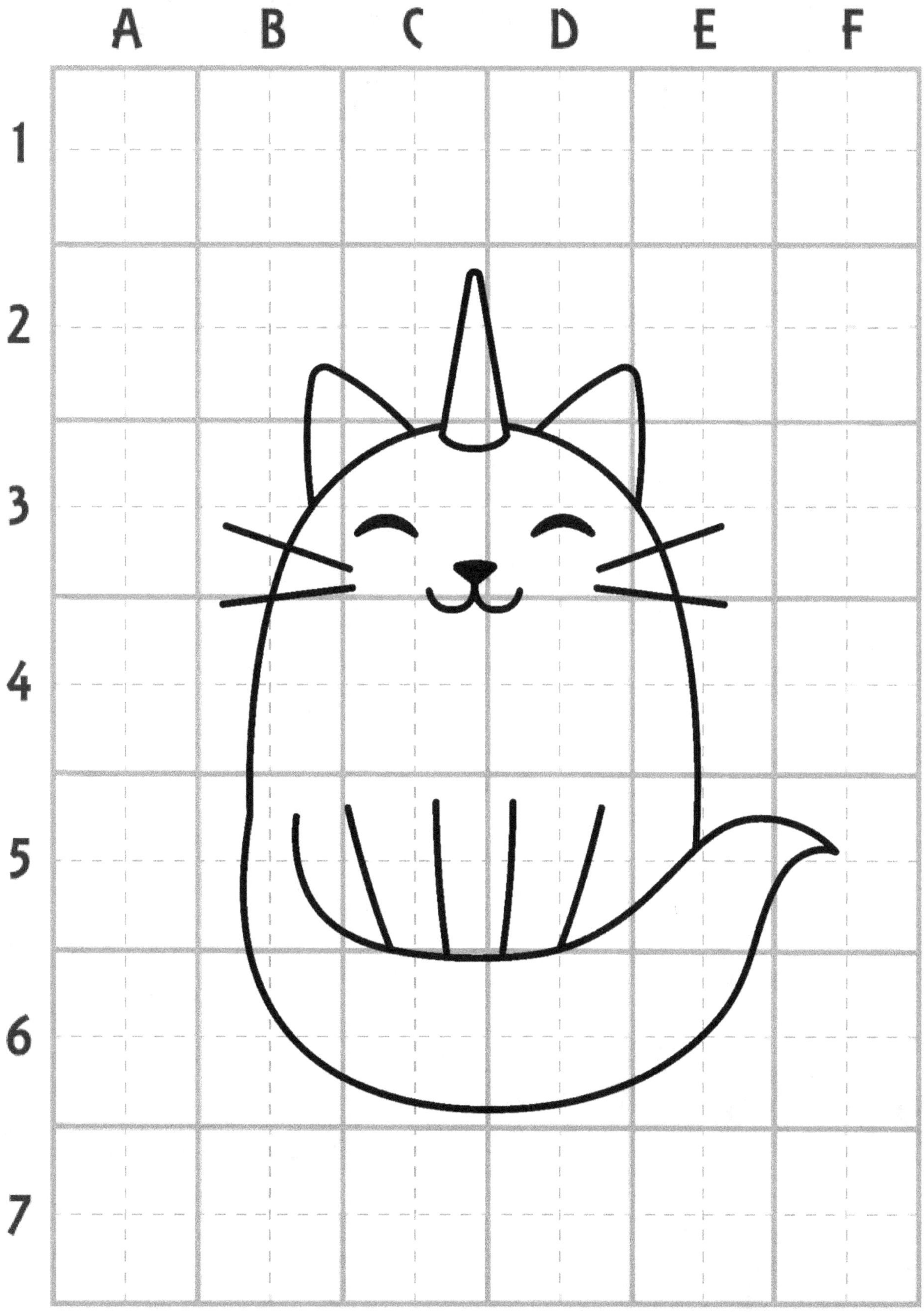
A
B
C
D
E
F
1
2
3
4
5
6
7

Your Turn!

	A	B	C	D	E	F
1						
2						
3						
4						
5						
6						
7						

Practice Makes Perfect!

Draw & Color

Practice Makes Perfect!

Draw & Color

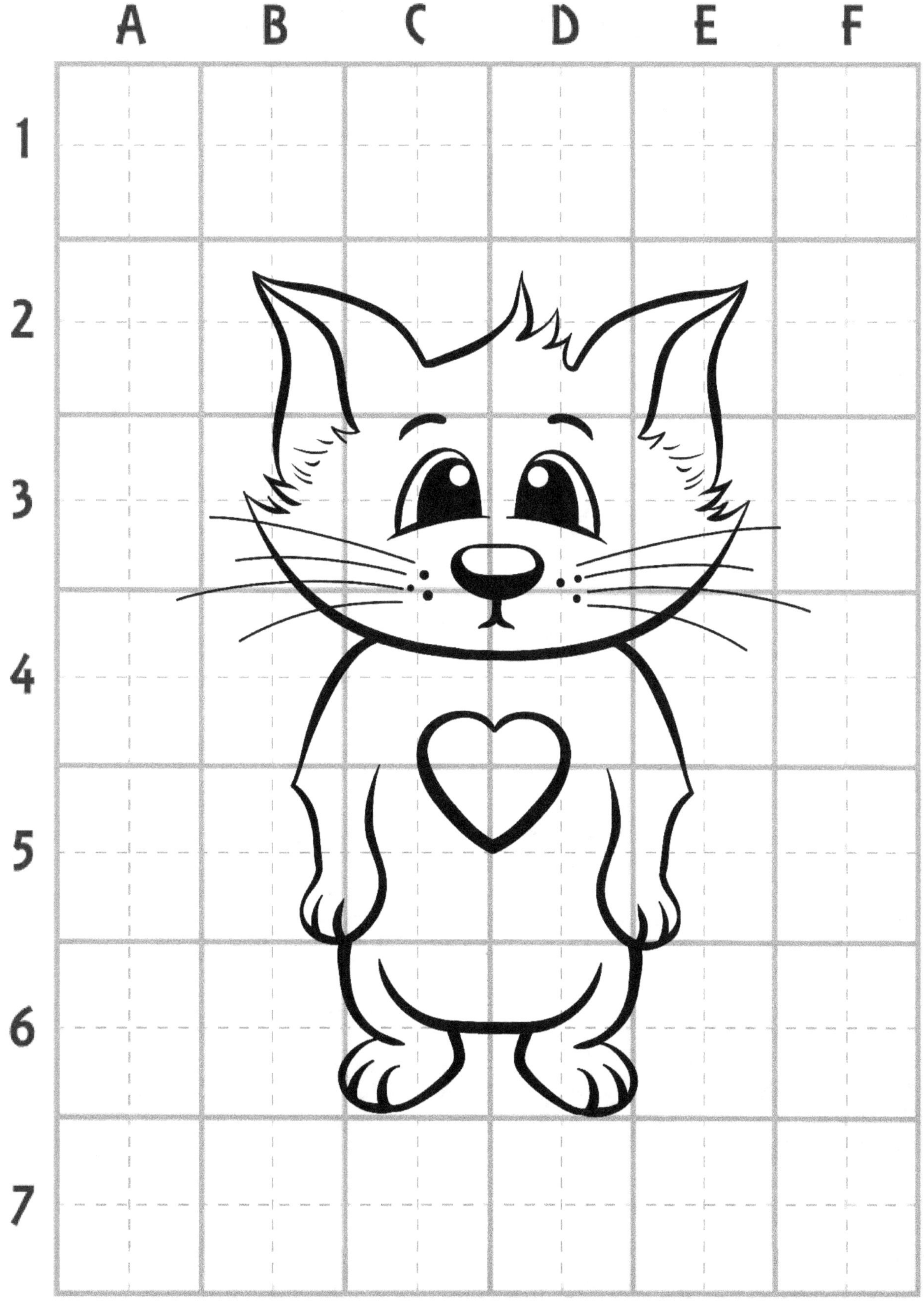
A
B
C
D
E
F
1
2
3
4
5
6
7

Your Turn!

	A	B	C	D	E	F
1						
2						
3						
4						
5						
6						
7						

Practice Makes Perfect!

Draw & Color

Practice Makes Perfect!

Draw & Color

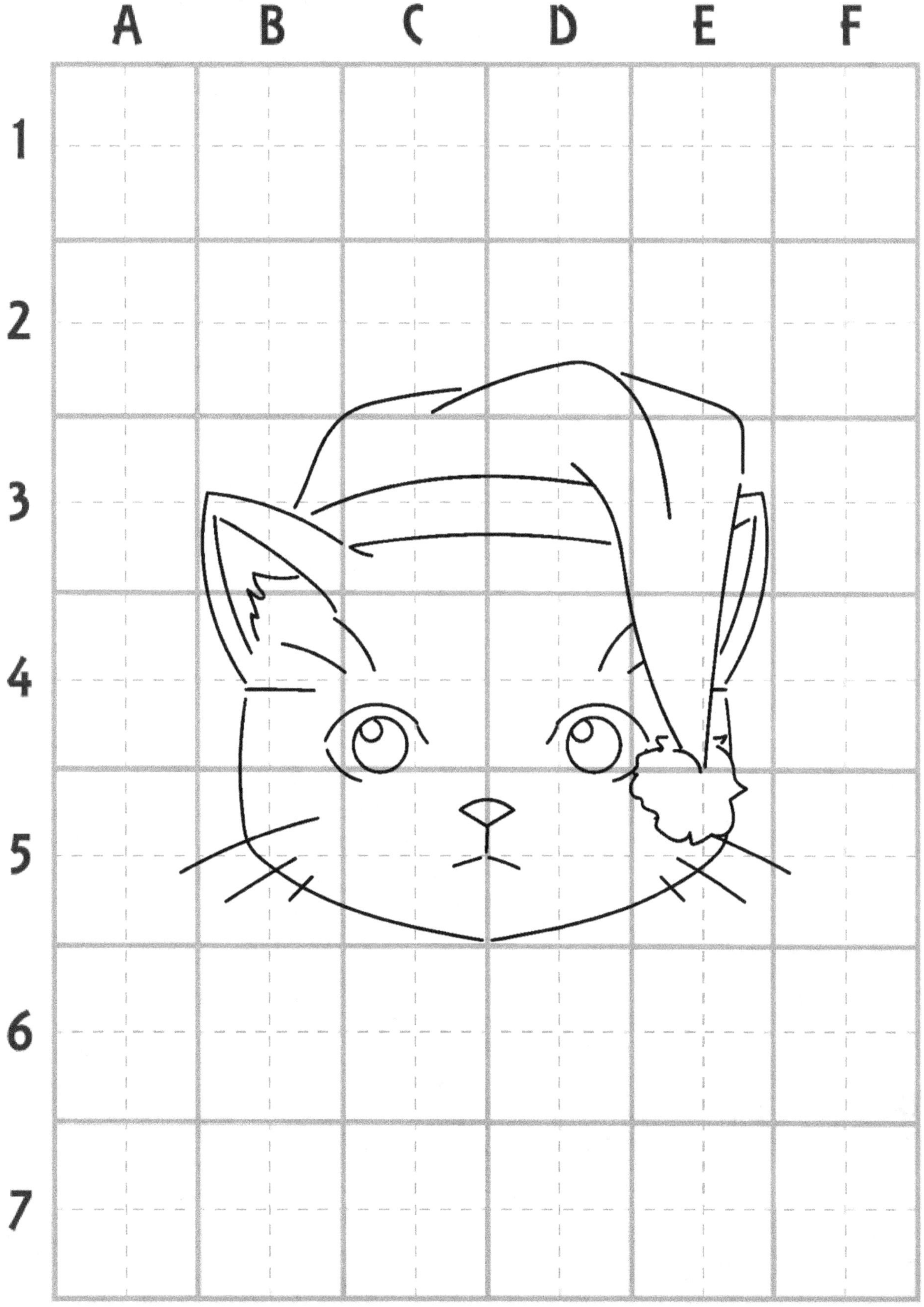
A
B
C
D
E
F
1
2
3
4
5
6
7

Your Turn!

	A	B	C	D	E	F
1						
2						
3						
4						
5						
6						
7						

Practice Makes Perfect!

Draw & Color

Practice Makes Perfect!

Draw & Color

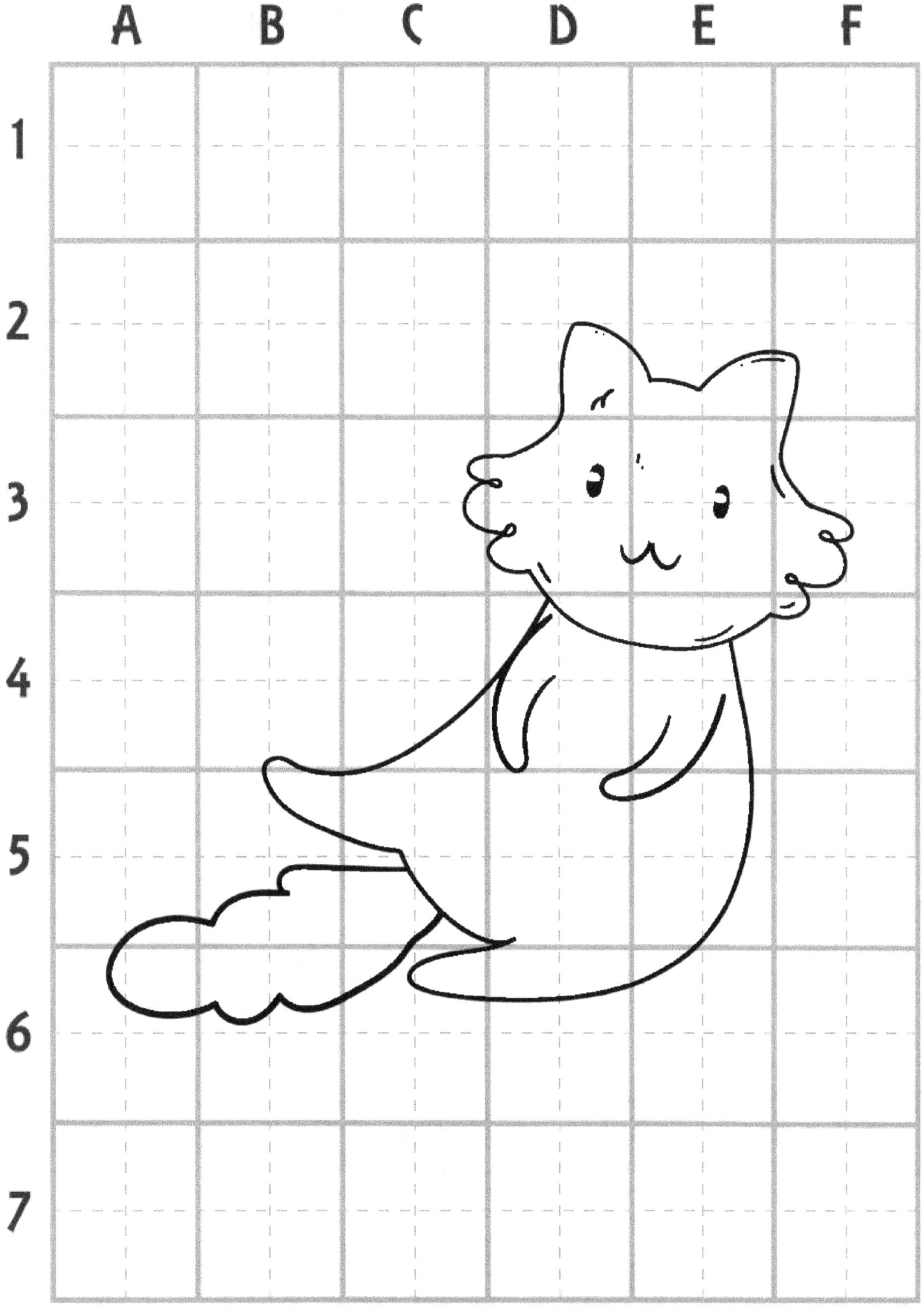
A B C D E F
1 2 3 4 5 6 7

Your Turn!

	A	B	C	D	E	F
1						
2						
3						
4						
5						
6						
7						

Practice Makes Perfect!

Draw & Color

Practice Makes Perfect!

Draw & Color

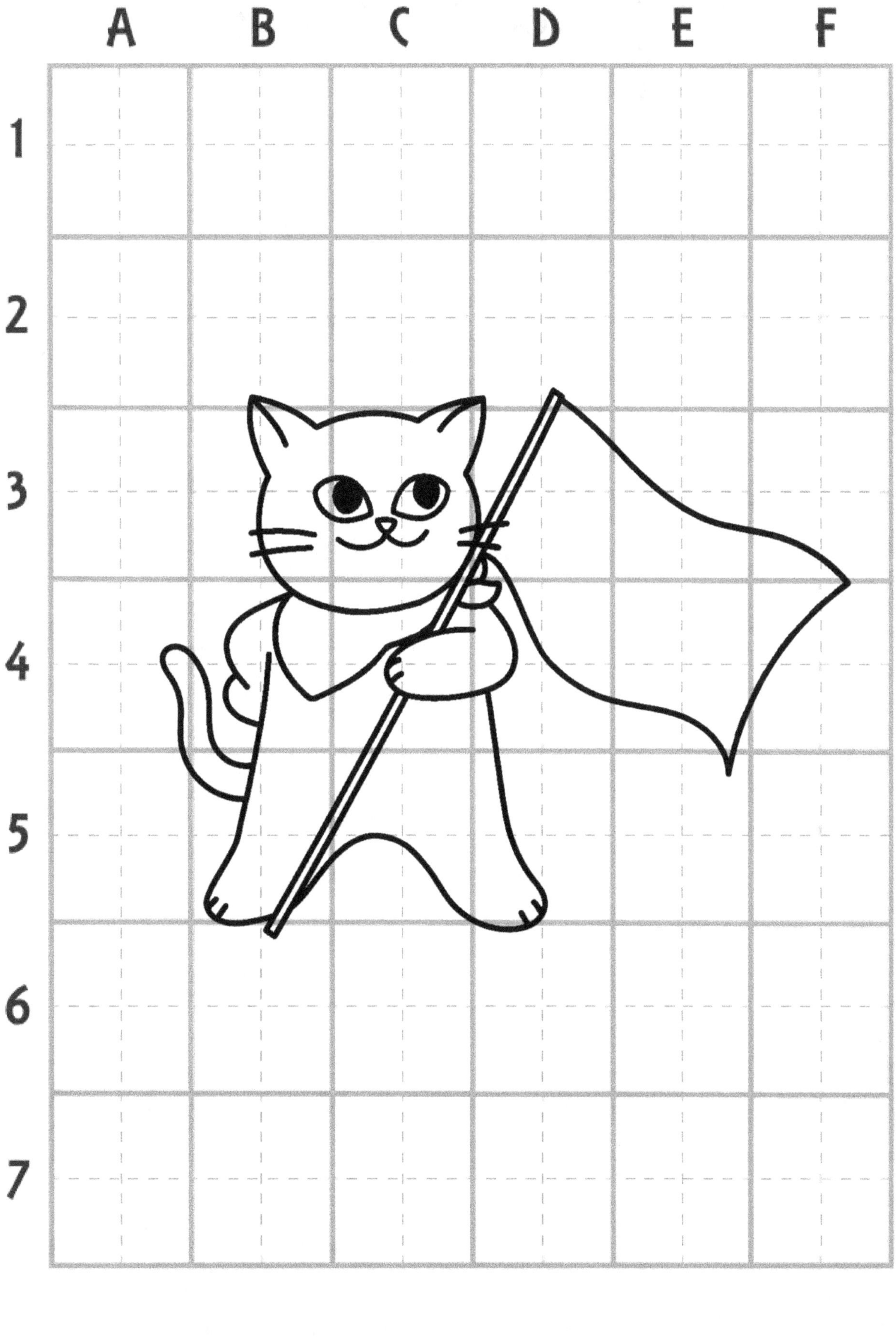
A
B
C
D
E
F
1
2
3
4
5
6
7

Your Turn!

	A	B	C	D	E	F
1						
2						
3						
4						
5						
6						
7						

Practice Makes Perfect!

Draw & Color

Practice Makes Perfect!

Draw & Color

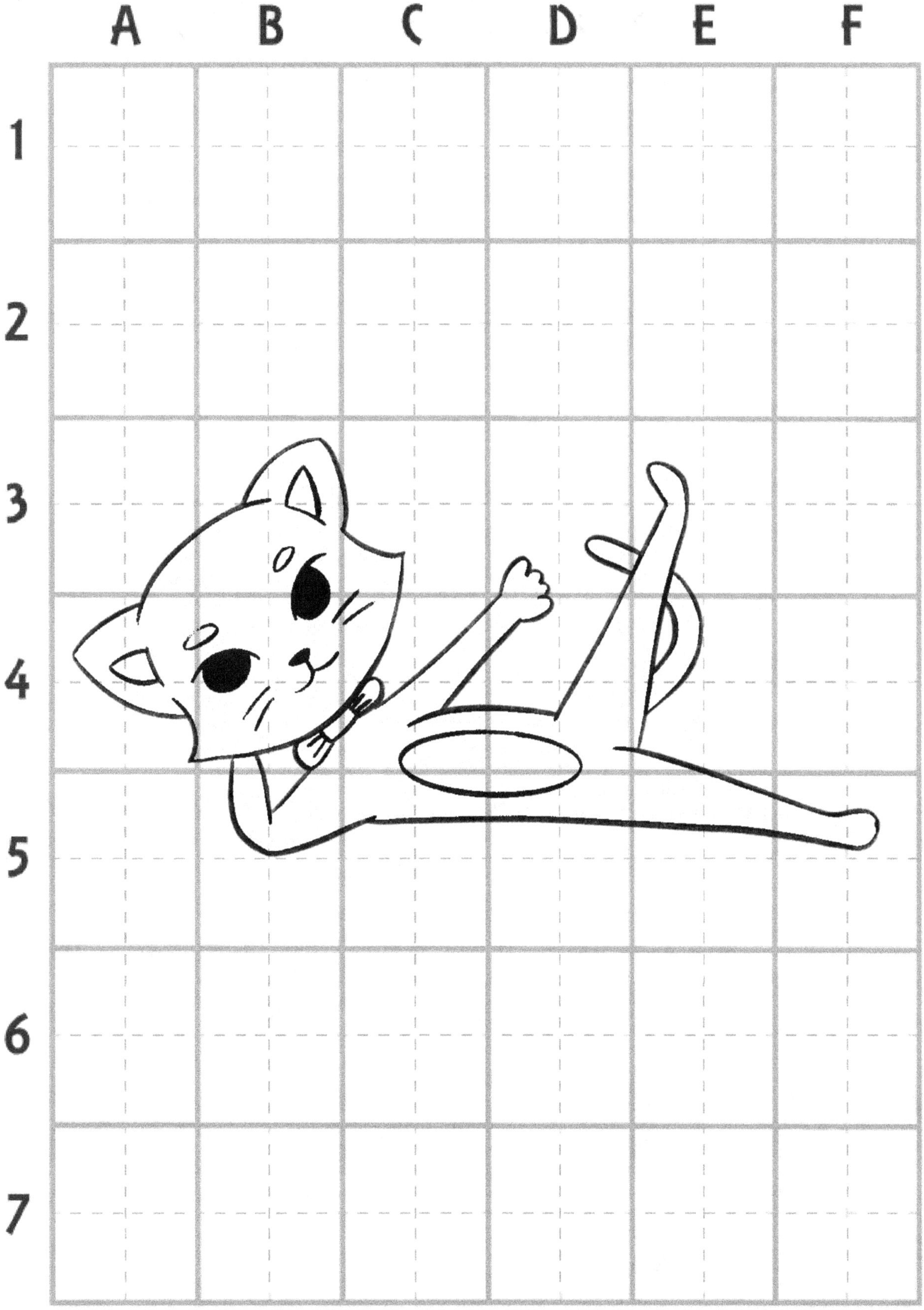
A B C D E F
1 2 3 4 5 6 7

Your Turn!

	A	B	C	D	E	F
1						
2						
3						
4						
5						
6						
7						

Practice Makes Perfect!

Draw & Color

Practice Makes Perfect!

Draw & Color

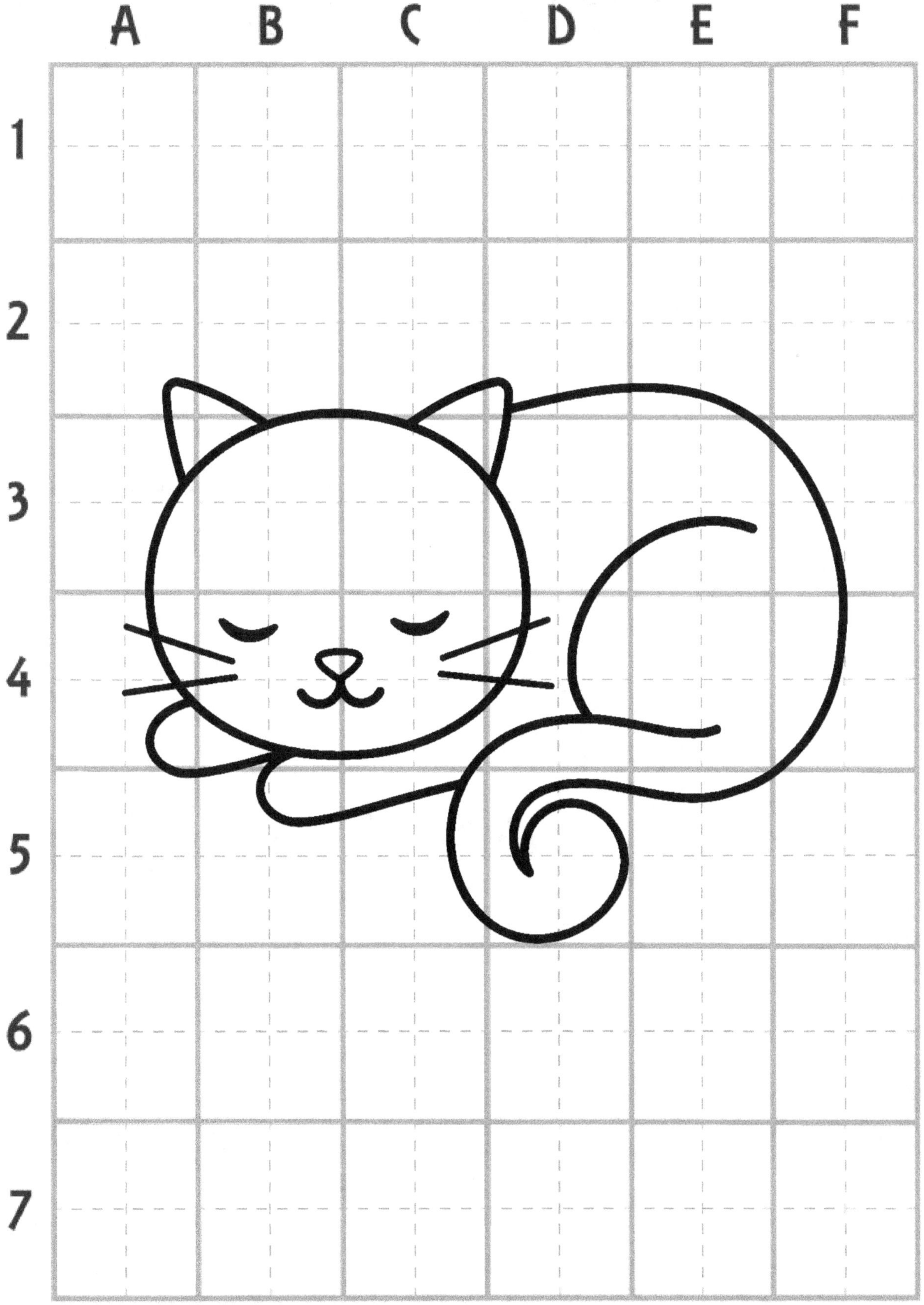
A
B
C
D
E
F
1
2
3
4
5
6
7

Your Turn!

	A	B	C	D	E	F
1						
2						
3						
4						
5						
6						
7						

Practice Makes Perfect!

Draw & Color

Practice Makes Perfect!

Draw & Color

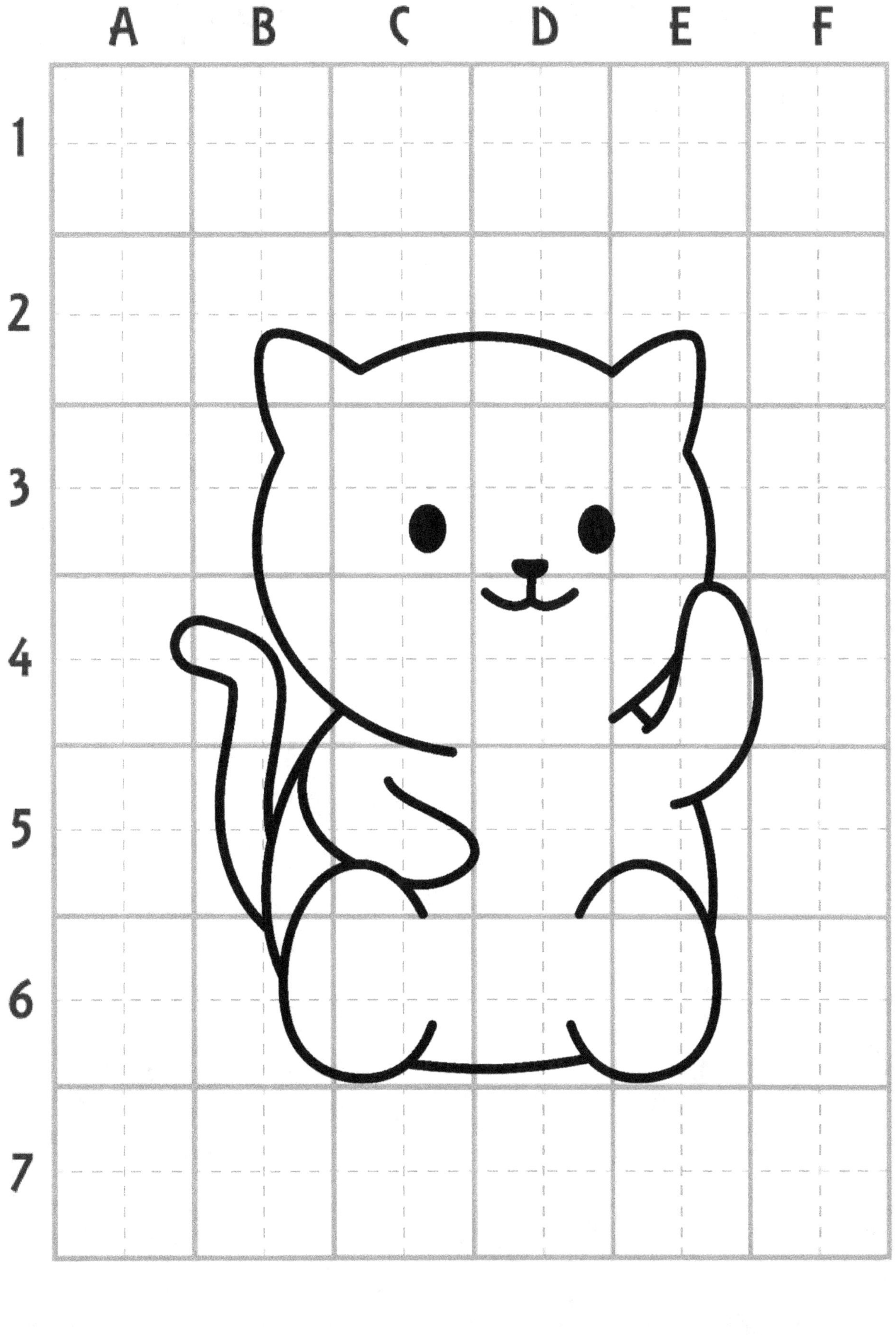
A
B
C
D
E
F
1
2
3
4
5
6
7

Your Turn!

	A	B	C	D	E	F
1						
2						
3						
4						
5						
6						
7						

Practice Makes Perfect!

Draw & Color

Practice Makes Perfect!

Draw & Color

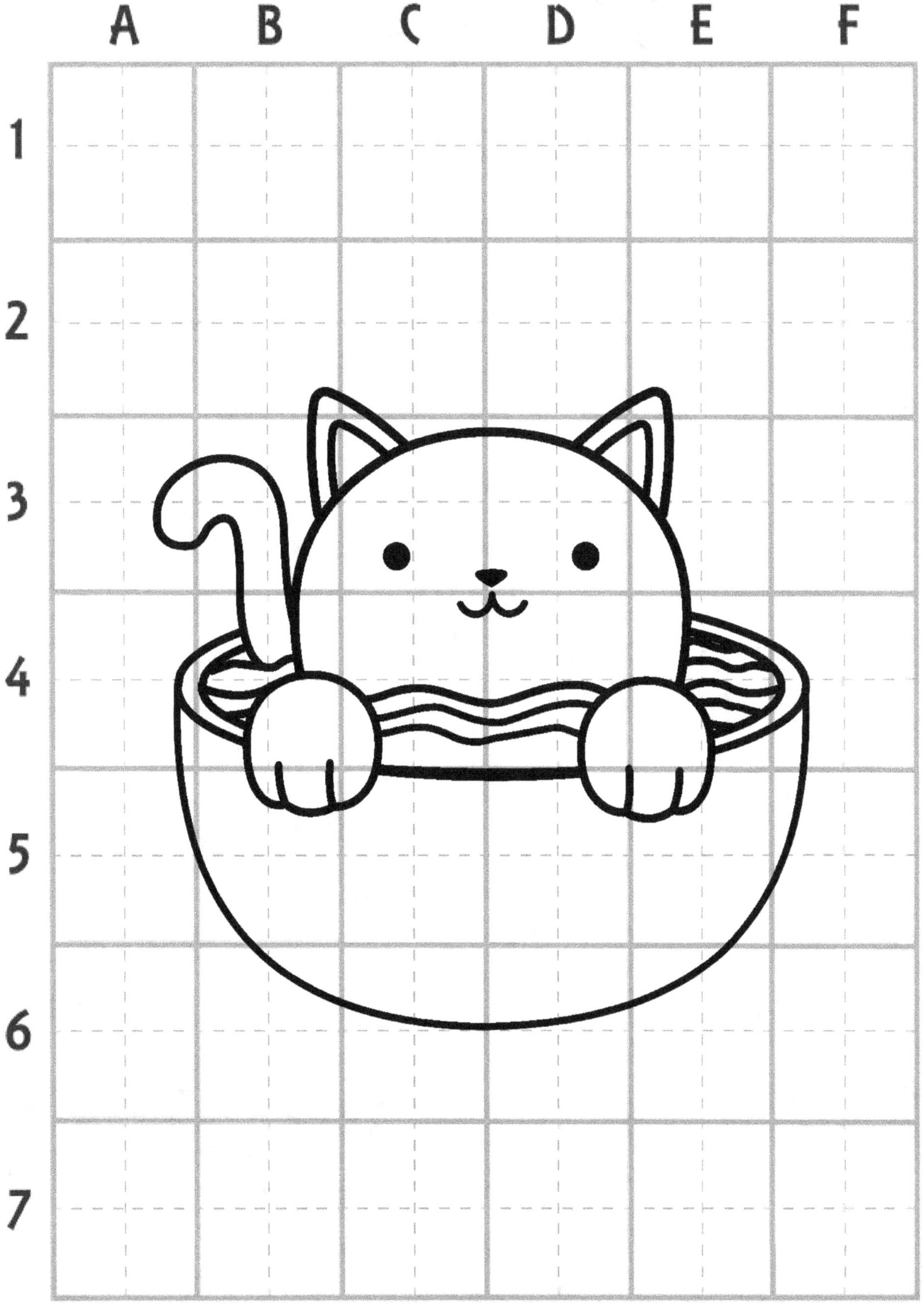
A B C D E F
1 2 3 4 5 6 7

Your Turn!

	A	B	C	D	E	F
1						
2						
3						
4						
5						
6						
7						

Practice Makes Perfect!

Draw & Color

Practice Makes Perfect!

Draw & Color

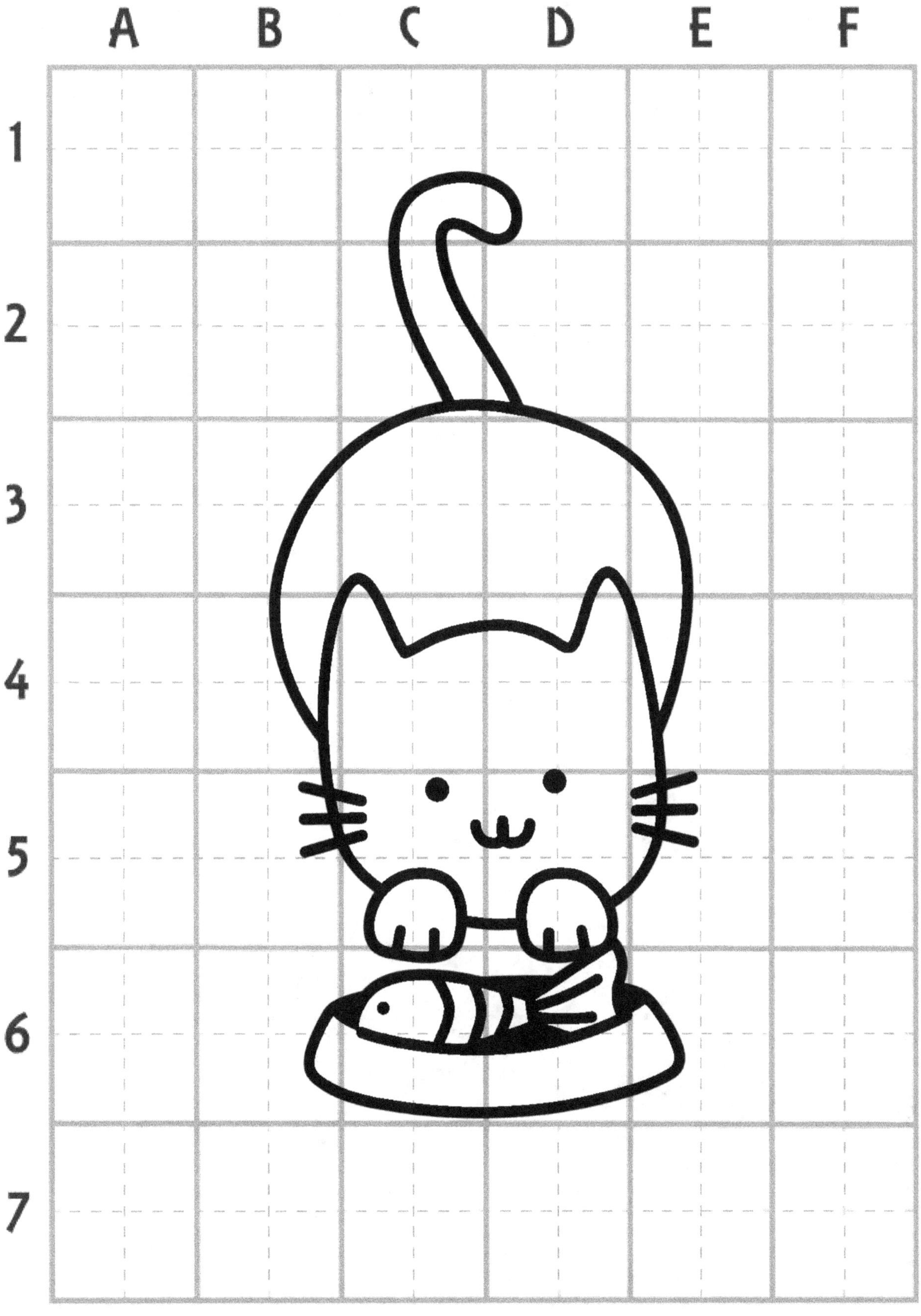
A
B
C
D
E
F
1
2
3
4
5
6
7

Your Turn!

	A	B	C	D	E	F
1						
2						
3						
4						
5						
6						
7						

Practice Makes Perfect!

Draw & Color

Practice Makes Perfect!

Draw & Color

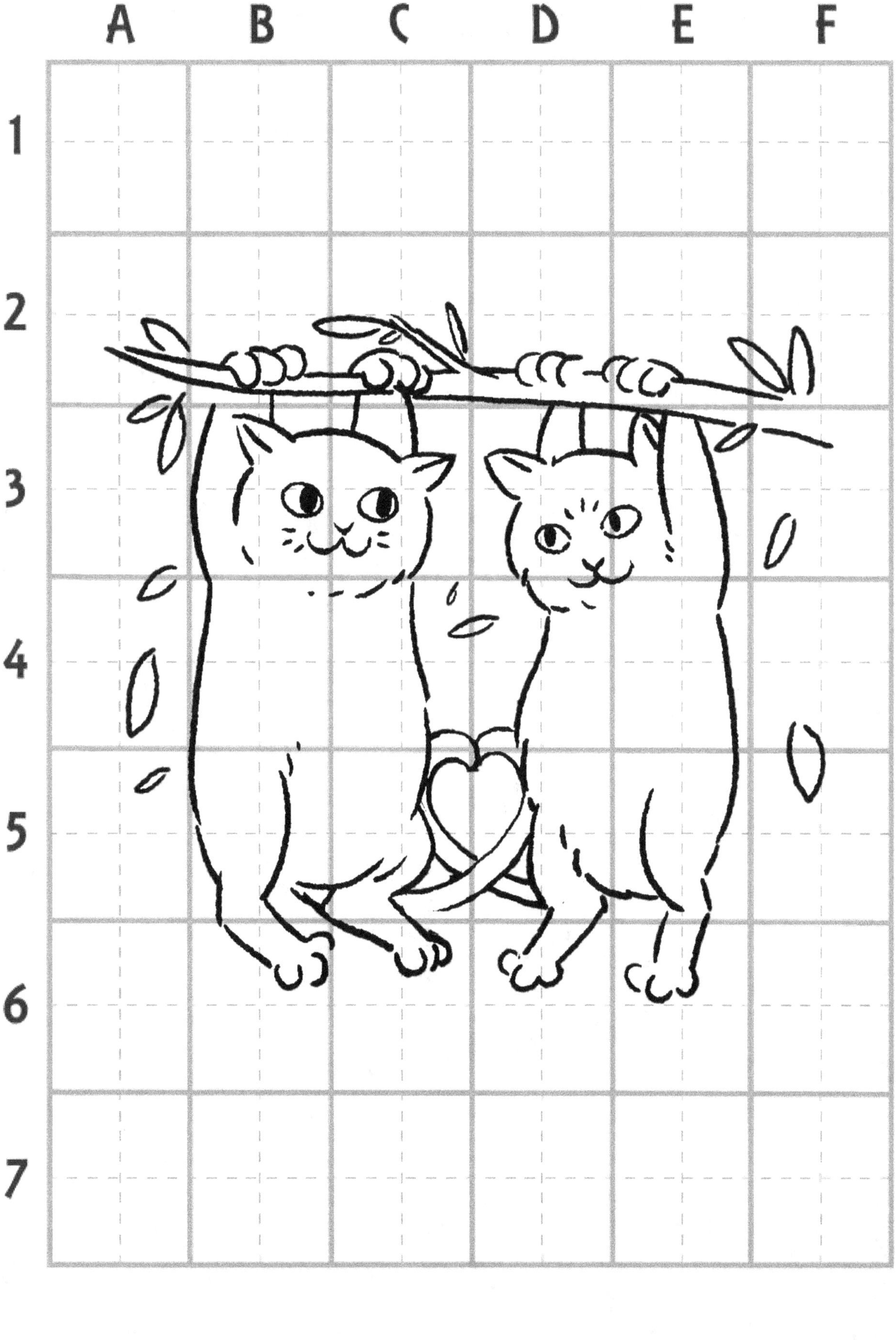
A B C D E F
1
2
3
4
5
6
7

Your Turn!

	A	B	C	D	E	F
1						
2						
3						
4						
5						
6						
7						

Practice Makes Perfect!

Draw & Color

Practice Makes Perfect!

Draw & Color

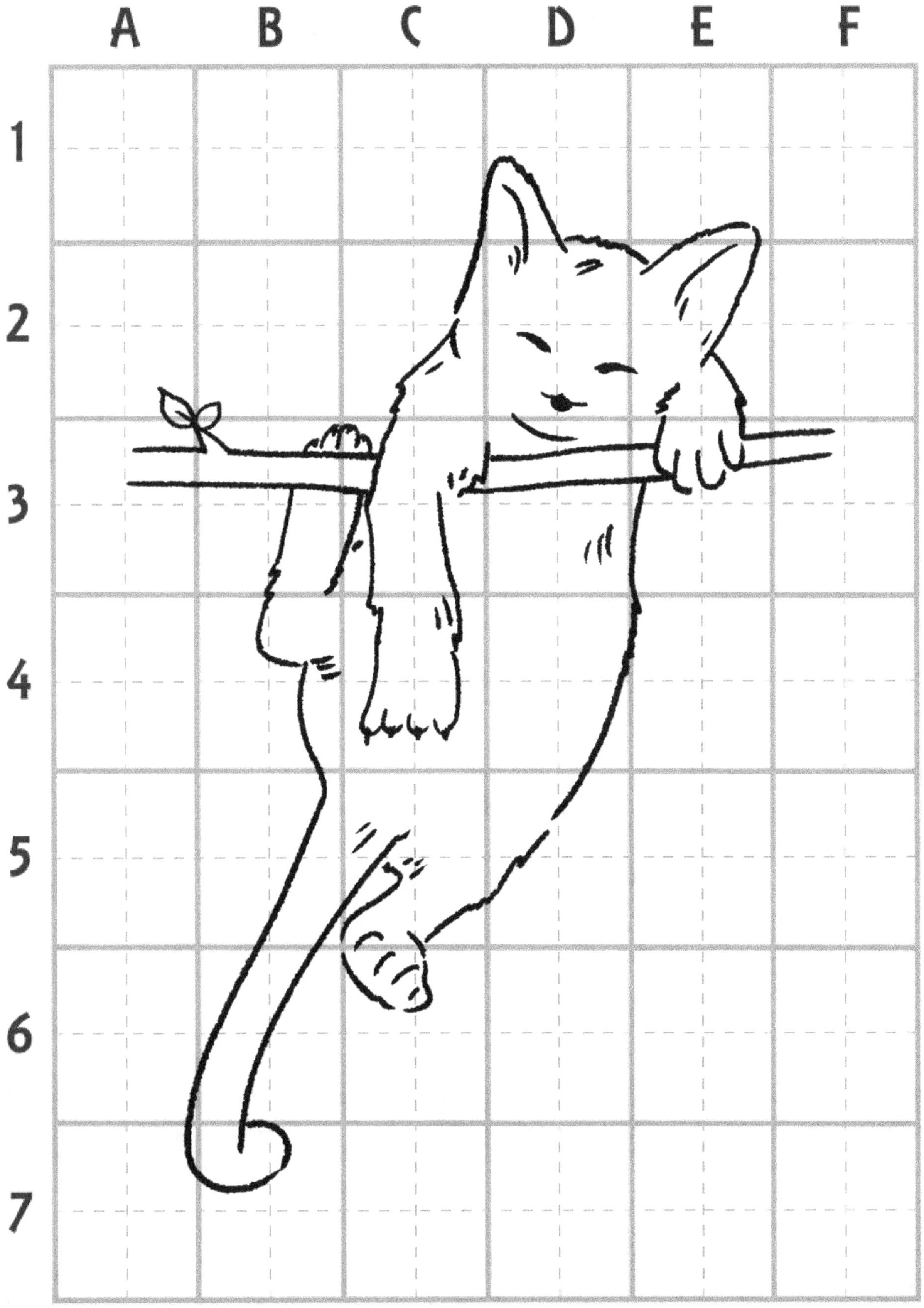
A
B
C
D
E
F
1
2
3
4
5
6
7

Your Turn!

	A	B	C	D	E	F
1						
2						
3						
4						
5						
6						
7						

Practice Makes Perfect!

Draw & Color

Practice Makes Perfect!

Draw & Color

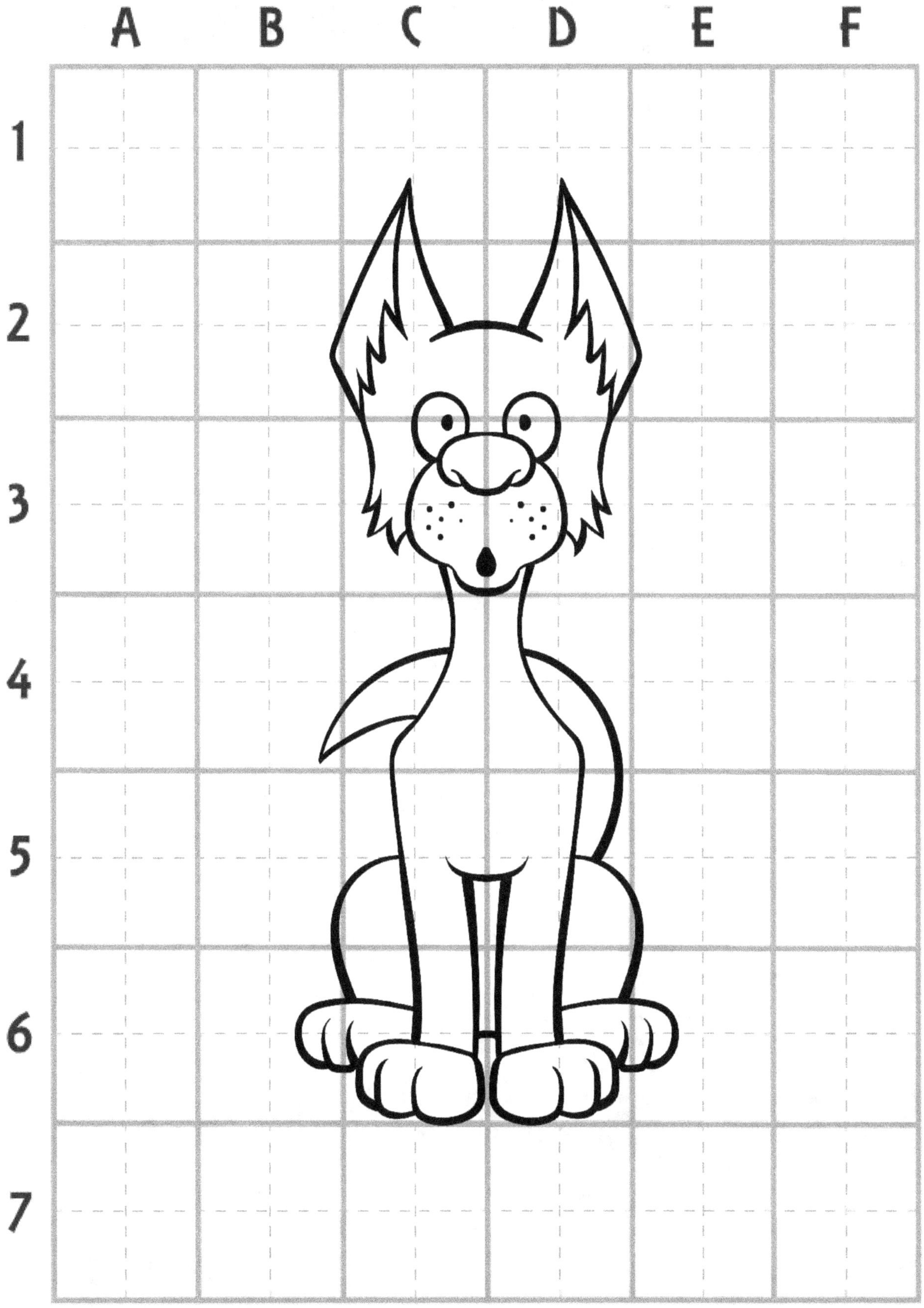

A B C D E F
1
2
3
4
5
6
7

Your Turn!

	A	B	C	D	E	F
1						
2						
3						
4						
5						
6						
7						

Practice Makes Perfect!

Draw & Color

Practice Makes Perfect!

Draw & Color

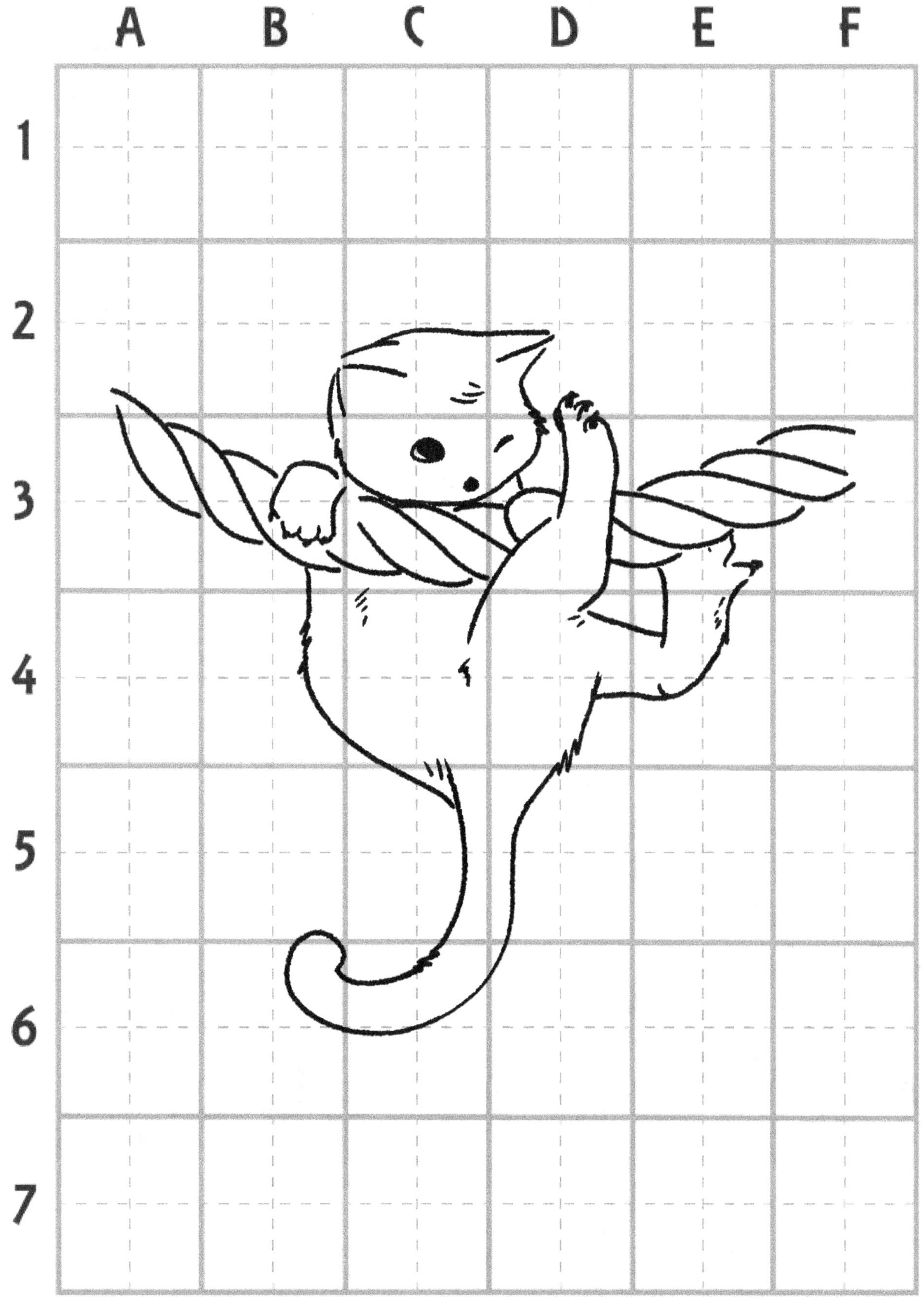
A
B
C
D
E
F
1
2
3
4
5
6
7

Your Turn!

	A	B	C	D	E	F
1						
2						
3						
4						
5						
6						
7						

Practice Makes Perfect!

Draw & Color

Practice Makes Perfect!

Draw & Color

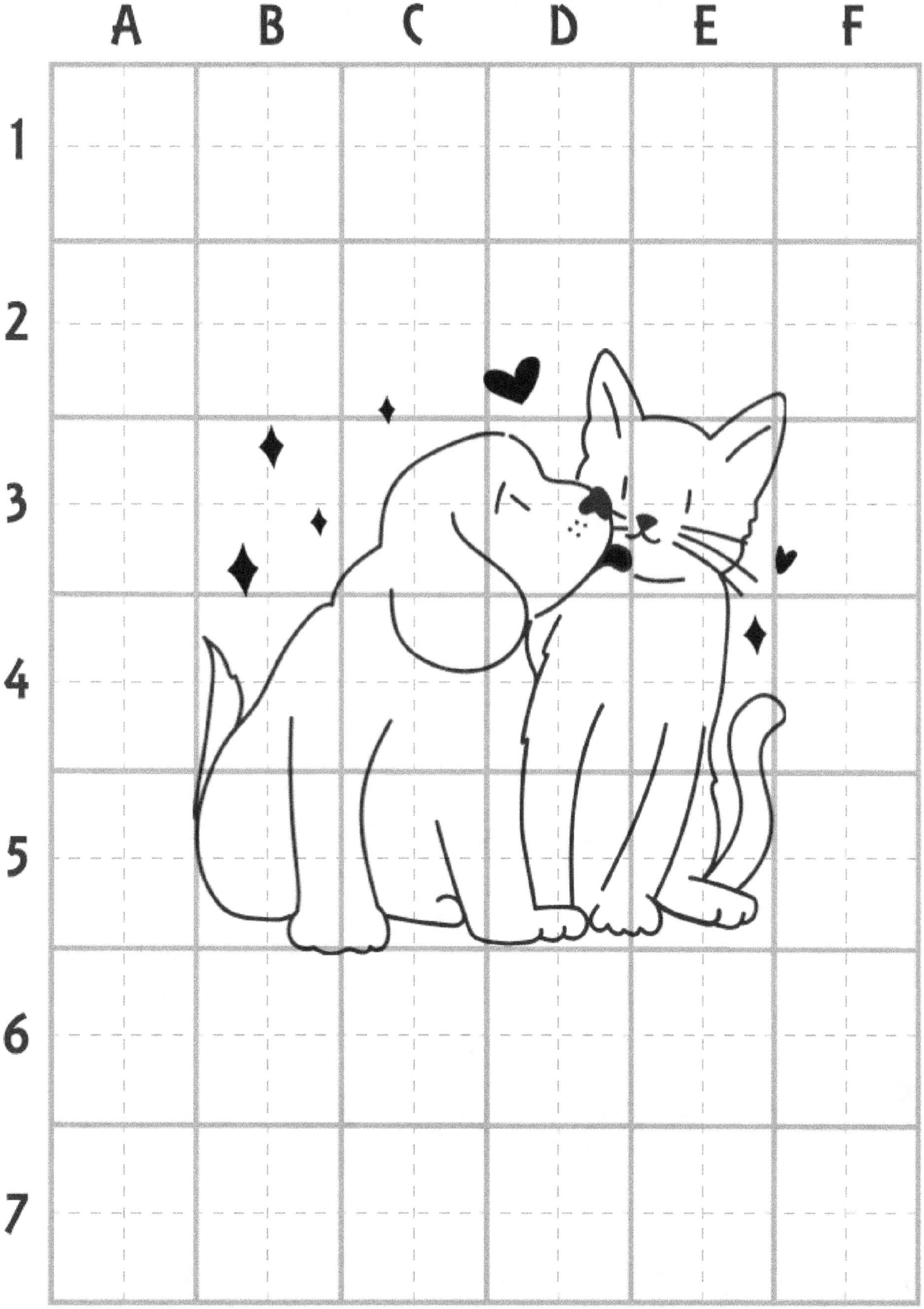
A B C D E F
1 2 3 4 5 6 7

Your Turn!

	A	B	C	D	E	F
1						
2						
3						
4						
5						
6						
7						

Practice Makes Perfect!

Draw & Color

Practice Makes Perfect!

Draw & Color

www.ingramcontent.com/pod-product-compliance
Lightning Source LLC
Chambersburg PA
CBHW080541220526
45466CB00010B/2991